Hyperdimensional Starseeds: Navigating Multiple Realities

Understanding the Complexity of Existing in Multiple Dimensions Simultaneously

Campbell Quinn McCarthy

Copyright © 2024 S.D.N Publishing

All rights reserved

ISBN: 9798875610837

The characters and events portrayed in this book are fictitious. Any similarity to real persons, living or dead, is coincidental and not intended by the author.

No part of this book may be reproduced, or stored in a retrieval system, or transmitted in any form or by any means, electronic, mechanical, photocopying, recording, or otherwise, without express written permission of the publisher.

General Disclaimer

This book is intended to provide informative and educational material on the subject matter covered. The author(s), publisher, and any affiliated parties make no representations or warranties with respect to the accuracy, applicability, completeness, or suitability of the contents herein and specifically disclaim any implied warranties of merchantability or fitness for a particular purpose.

The information contained in this book is for general information purposes only and is not intended to serve as legal, medical, financial, or any other form of professional advice. Readers should consult with appropriate professionals before making any decisions based on the information provided. Neither the author(s) nor the publisher shall be held responsible or liable for any loss, damage, injury, claim, or otherwise, whether direct or indirect, consequential, or incidental, that may occur as a result of applying or misinterpreting the information in this book.

This book may contain references to third-party websites, products, or services. Such references do not constitute an endorsement or recommendation, and the author(s) and publisher are not responsible for any outcomes related to these third-party references.

In no event shall the author(s), publisher, or any affiliated parties be liable for any direct, indirect, punitive, special, incidental, or other consequential damages arising

HYPERDIMENSIONAL STARSEEDS: NAVIGATING...

directly or indirectly from any use of this material, which is provided "as is," and without warranties of any kind, express or implied.

By reading this book, you acknowledge and agree that you assume all risks and responsibilities concerning the applicability and consequences of the information provided. You also agree to indemnify, defend, and hold harmless the author(s), publisher, and any affiliated parties from any and all liabilities, claims, demands, actions, and causes of action whatsoever, whether or not foreseeable, that may arise from using or misusing the information contained in this book.

Although every effort has been made to ensure the accuracy of the information in this book as of the date of publication, the landscape of the subject matter covered is continuously evolving. Therefore, the author(s) and publisher expressly disclaim responsibility for any errors or omissions and reserve the right to update, alter, or revise the content without prior notice.

By continuing to read this book, you agree to be bound by the terms and conditions stated in this disclaimer. If you do not agree with these terms, it is your responsibility to discontinue use of this book immediately.

Contents

1. Unlocking the Mysteries of Hyperdimensional Existence — 1
2. Foundational Concepts — 5
3. Starseeds and Dimensions — 22
4. Tools for Hyperdimensional Travel — 40
5. Interacting with Parallel Universes — 60
6. Starseeds and Time-Space Reality — 80
7. Energy Work and Hyperdimensions — 98
8. Spiritual and Cosmic Laws — 114
9. Starseed Missions and Hyperdimensions — 130
10. Galactic Heritage and Lineages — 144
11. Psychic Abilities and Multidimensional Perception — 158
12. Hyperdimensional Relationships — 177
13. Challenges and Solutions — 198
14. Philosophical Perspectives — 219

| 15. | Starseed Activations and Upgrades | 236 |
| 16. | Final Reflections and Considerations | 253 |

Unlocking the Mysteries of Hyperdimensional Existence

Embark on a transcendent journey through the entwined realms of science and spirituality as we venture into the enigmatic world of hyperdimensional existence. This odyssey transcends the conventional boundaries of perception, inviting you to explore the profound depths of multidimensional consciousness. "Hyperdimensional Starseeds: Navigating Multiple Realities" is a meticulously crafted guide, offering lucid insights into the esoteric concept of existing simultaneously across multiple dimensions.

At the crux of this exploration lies the concept of 'Starseeds' - sentient entities believed to originate beyond the confines of earthly existence, embodying a cosmic legacy and purpose. This book delves deep into the fabric of dimensional theory, unraveling the intricate tapestry that weaves together the science of reality, the nature of consciousness, and the phenomenon of hyperdimensions.

As you navigate through the subsequent chapters, each carefully structured segment unravels the complexities of how Starseeds experience dimensions, their unique genetic codes, and their multifaceted selves. From examining the role of sacred geometry in dimensional travel to understanding the interplay of Starseeds with parallel universes, this book paints a comprehensive picture of a reality far more intricate than the one perceived by our five senses.

Particularly intriguing is the exploration of tools for hyperdimensional travel, offering practical guidance on sacred geometry, crystal usage, and advanced meditation techniques. As the journey progresses, the discussion shifts to the fascinating realms of interacting with parallel universes, delving into the Mandela Effect, time loops, and the enchanting nature of synchronicity.

In the heart of the book lies the intricate relationship between Starseeds and the time-space reality, a topic that bridges the gap between quantum mechanics and spirituality. As you immerse yourself in the theoretical expanse of the Unified Field Theory, temporal mechanics, and the multi-layered essence of time as a dimension, you'll find yourself at the precipice of a new understanding of your place in the cosmos.

Furthermore, the book offers a profound exploration of energy work within hyperdimensions, discussing Kundalini energy, chakra systems, and the subtle intricacies of your energetic aura. As you dive deeper, the spiritual and cosmic laws governing hyperdimensional existence unfold before you, shedding light on the Law of Attraction, karmic influences, and the principle of cosmic justice.

The latter chapters of this work are dedicated to the missions and galactic heritage of Starseeds, as well as the development and nurturing of psychic abilities within the multidimensional spectrum. An intimate examination of hyperdimensional relationships reveals the complexity of soul contracts, twin flames, and the cosmic family tree, providing a profound understanding of the interconnectedness of all beings across dimensions.

Yet, the journey is not without its challenges. As we navigate through dimensional shifts and psychic protections, the book provides compassionate guidance and solutions to help overcome the hurdles inherent in hyperdimensional existence. Finally, philosophical perspectives offer a contemplative lens through which to view quantum mechanics, free will, and the nature of duality across dimensions.

As the expedition through this enigmatic realm concludes, we are bestowed with practical insights and reflections on our ancient wisdom, cosmic legacy, and the interconnected cosmic web that binds us all. "Hyperdimensional Starseeds: Navigating Multiple Realities" is more than a book; it is a beacon, a compass for those yearning to step into their hyperdimensional power, transcend limitations, and embrace their multidimensional journey with light and wisdom.

In the chapters that follow, prepare to unravel the tapestry of existence, to journey beyond the visible spectrum of reality, and to discover the cosmic dance that interlinks all facets of existence across dimensions. May this voyage enlighten, empower, and transform your understanding of the cosmos and your place within it.

Foundational Concepts

What are Starseeds?

In the quest to understand the vastness of our universe, the concept of Starseeds presents a captivating paradigm, challenging the very essence of our understanding of identity and existence. Let's dive straight into the heart of what constitutes a Starseed, exploring their origins, characteristics, and the profound implications of their presence in our multidimensional reality.

Origins and Nature of Starseeds

The term 'Starseed' can be likened to a cosmic seed planted in the fertile ground of the universe. These are beings believed to originate from different star systems, galaxies, or dimensional realities. Their essence is not just confined to the physicality of one planet or dimension but spans across the cosmos. The purpose of Starseeds is often viewed as a mission to bring knowledge, aid in spiritual awakening, and foster a deeper connection between the Earth and other cosmic entities.

The origins of Starseeds are shrouded in mystery and are often the subject of extensive metaphysical speculation. Some theories suggest that they are souls incarnated on Earth from other worlds, chosen or volunteered for the purpose of aiding the planet in its evolutionary journey. Others believe that Starseeds are a manifestation of the universe's consciousness, seeking to experience itself through different forms and dimensions.

Characteristics of Starseeds

Starseeds are often distinguished by a sense of alienation or difference, sensing from a young age that they do not entirely belong to the world they find themselves in. This is not just a feeling of social or cultural dissonance but a deeper, more intrinsic sense of being 'otherworldly'. Common characteristics among Starseeds include:

- **Empathic Abilities**: A heightened sense of empathy, allowing them to deeply perceive and sometimes absorb the emotions of others.

- **Spiritual Yearning**: An innate drive towards understanding the mysteries of the universe, often accompanied by an interest in metaphysics, spirituality, and other realms of existence.

- **Sense of Mission**: A profound feeling that they are here to fulfill a specific purpose, often related to healing, teaching, or guiding humanity towards a higher consciousness.

The Role of Starseeds in Human Evolution

The purported mission of Starseeds is deeply interwoven with the evolution of consciousness on Earth. They are thought to be harbingers of change, bringing with them new perspectives, ideas, and energies that challenge and expand our current understanding of reality. Their role is often seen as a catalytic one, accelerating spiritual awakening and fostering a greater sense of interconnectedness among all beings.

In the broader cosmic narrative, Starseeds are believed to play a crucial role in bridging the gap between the physical and metaphysical realms. By grounding higher-dimensional energies into the Earth plane, they contribute to the vibrational upliftment of the planet, aiding in its transition to a higher state of consciousness.

Starseeds and Their Connection to Multiple Realities

One of the most fascinating aspects of Starseeds is their inherent connection to multiple dimensions of existence. They are often described as having the ability to navigate different realms of consciousness, enabling them to access wisdom and knowledge from various sources. This multi-dimensional awareness allows them to perceive reality through a unique lens, often leading to profound spiritual insights and innovations.

We have developed the foundational understanding of what it means to be a Starseed, setting the stage for a deeper exploration of their experiences and roles in subsequent chapters. As we delve further into the nature of Starseeds, we begin to unravel the intricate tapestry of cosmic consciousness and its manifestation in our multidimensional universe.

Starseeds are not just a concept or a metaphor but represent a significant aspect of our evolving understanding of the universe. They challenge us to expand our perception beyond the confines of traditional thought and open our minds to the vast possibilities of existence. As we continue our journey through this book, we invite you to keep an open heart and mind, allowing the mysteries of the cosmos to unfold in their majestic complexity.

Introduction to Dimensional Theory

In our exploration of hyperdimensional existence, a fundamental understanding of dimensional theory is imperative. Therefore let's introduce the concepts and principles that underpin our perception of dimensions and how they relate to the multifaceted experience of Starseeds. The dimensional theory is not just a scientific concept but also a spiritual and metaphysical one, offering a window into the complexities of the universe and our place within it.

Understanding Dimensions

At its core, dimensional theory pertains to the various levels or layers of reality that exist beyond our immediate sensory perception. Traditionally, we perceive our world in three dimensions - length, width, and height. However, dimensional theory suggests that there are additional, unseen dimensions interwoven with our reality.

In physics, particularly in string theory, dimensions beyond the familiar three are proposed to explain the fundamental forces of the universe and the nature of particles. However, in metaphysical discussions, dimensions are often viewed as different levels of consciousness or vibrational frequencies. Each dimension is thought to have its own unique characteristics and laws, offering a distinct way of experiencing reality.

The Multidimensional Universe

The concept of a multidimensional universe suggests that reality is not linear or confined to the three dimensions we commonly understand. Instead, it proposes an intricate tapestry of interconnected dimensions, each existing simultaneously and interdependently. This perspective is crucial in understanding the hyperdimensional nature of Starseeds, who are believed to be able to perceive, interact with, or even traverse these various dimensions.

In this view, dimensions are not just physical spaces but can also represent varying states of consciousness. For instance, the fourth dimension is often associated with time and the fifth with a higher, more spiritually awakened state of being. These higher dimensions are thought to be realms of greater enlightenment and understanding, where one can experience a profound connection with the universal energy and consciousness.

Dimensional Interplay and Starseeds

For Starseeds, the notion of dimensional interplay is central to their existence and purpose. They are often described as beings who have a natural affinity with higher dimensions, enabling them to access insights and knowledge that are not readily available in the third dimension. This ability allows them to act as bridges between dimensions, facilitating a greater flow of energy and consciousness across different levels of reality.

Starseeds' connection to higher dimensions is also believed to empower them with unique abilities and insights. These can manifest in various forms, such as heightened intuition, psychic abilities, or a deeper understanding of the spiritual laws that govern the universe. By tapping into the energies of higher dimensions, Starseeds can help to elevate the collective consciousness of humanity, guiding it towards a more enlightened and harmonious state.

Dimensional theory provides a framework for understanding the intricate and multi-layered nature of reality. It suggests that our universe is much more complex than what our physical senses perceive and that there are realms of existence beyond our ordinary experience. For Starseeds, this theory is not just an intellectual concept but a lived reality, offering them a unique perspective on life and the universe. As we delve deeper into the nature of hyperdimensional existence, the insights provided by dimensional theory will serve as a guiding light, helping us to navigate the unseen realms of the cosmos.

The Science of Reality: A Brief Overview

In our journey to understand the hyperdimensional nature of Starseeds and their interaction with multiple realities, it is essential to grasp the basic scientific principles that underlie our understanding of reality. So let's try to shed light on the fundamental concepts of reality from a scientific perspective, weaving them with the metaphysical aspects to provide a holistic view. By bridging the gap between science and spirituality, we can gain a more comprehensive understanding of the universe and our place within it.

The Fabric of Reality

The concept of reality in scientific terms is a complex and ever-evolving subject. At its core, it involves understanding the nature of matter, energy, space, and time. Traditional physics viewed reality as a three-dimensional space, governed by predictable laws and linear time. However, the advent of quantum physics has dramatically altered this view, introducing a reality that is far less predictable and far more intertwined with the observer's consciousness.

Quantum mechanics, a fundamental theory in physics, provides a framework for understanding the smallest particles in the universe – atoms and subatomic particles. It reveals a reality where particles can exist in multiple states simultaneously (quantum superposition) and be entangled over vast distances (quantum entanglement). This challenges our conventional notions of space and time, suggesting a reality that is deeply interconnected and not confined to the linear, three-dimensional space we experience in everyday life.

The Role of Consciousness

The intersection of consciousness with the fabric of reality is one of the most intriguing and debated topics in both science and spirituality. In quantum theory, the observer effect postulates that the act of observation can affect the outcome of an experiment, hinting at a profound link between consciousness and physical reality.

In the realm of metaphysics, consciousness is often seen as the primary substance of the universe, with matter and energy being manifestations of consciousness at different vibrational frequencies. This perspective views reality as a projection or manifestation of consciousness, with each individual's perception of reality being a unique expression of their consciousness.

Hyperdimensional Realities

The concept of hyperdimensional realities extends beyond the boundaries of conventional science, delving into the realms of higher dimensions and alternate realities. In this context, higher dimensions are not just spatial dimensions but also dimensions of consciousness, each with its own set of laws and perceptions of reality.

Starseeds, as discussed in previous chapters, are believed to have a natural affinity with these higher dimensions, enabling them to perceive and interact with realities beyond the common three-dimensional space. This ability allows them to access wisdom and insights from these higher realms, aiding in their mission to elevate the consciousness of humanity and facilitate spiritual evolution.

The science of reality, particularly through the lens of quantum mechanics, offers a fascinating glimpse into the complexities and mysteries of the universe. It challenges us to expand our understanding of reality beyond the physical and tangible, into the realms of consciousness and higher dimensions. For Starseeds and those exploring the hyperdimensional aspects of existence, this scientific foundation provides a crucial context for understanding their experiences and the nature of the multiverse they navigate.

Understanding Hyperdimensions

The concept of hyperdimensions extends beyond the familiar three-dimensional space and time, inviting us to explore realms of existence that defy our conventional understanding of reality. Let's delve into the complex and fascinating world of hyperdimensions, shedding light on their nature, significance, and the role they play in the context of Starseeds and their multidimensional experiences.

The Nature of Hyperdimensions

Hyperdimensions refer to dimensions beyond the commonly perceived three-dimensional space and the fourth dimension of time. In the realm of theoretical physics, these higher dimensions are crucial in theories like string theory, which posits the existence of up to ten or eleven dimensions to explain the fundamental forces and particles in the universe.

In metaphysical and spiritual contexts, however, hyperdimensions are often associated with higher states of consciousness and spiritual realms. Each higher dimension is believed to operate at a higher vibrational frequency and encompasses a broader perspective of reality. These dimensions are not just places or destinations but states of being, offering profound insights into the nature of existence, consciousness, and the interconnectedness of all things.

Hyperdimensions and Consciousness

The exploration of hyperdimensions inevitably leads to a discussion about consciousness. In hyperdimensional spaces, consciousness is not limited to the physical body or the linear progression of time. Instead, it expands, allowing access to higher wisdom, knowledge, and spiritual truths.

Starseeds, in particular, are thought to have a natural affinity with these higher dimensions, enabling them to perceive and interact with these realms in ways that most people cannot. Their consciousness is attuned in such a way that they can navigate through these dimensions, bringing back insights and energies that can aid in the spiritual evolution of humanity.

Starseeds and Hyperdimensional Travel

For Starseeds, travel through hyperdimensions is more than just a physical journey; it is an exploration of consciousness and a journey of the soul. This form of travel allows them to connect with their higher selves, access past and future aspects of their existence, and communicate with other entities and consciousnesses within these higher realms.

Hyperdimensional travel can manifest in various forms, including astral projection, remote viewing, or through deep meditative states. In these states, Starseeds can traverse different dimensions, gaining insights that are not bound by the limitations of physical reality. This ability plays a crucial role in their mission on Earth, as it allows them to bring back knowledge and energy that can help in raising the planet's vibrational frequency.

Understanding hyperdimensions is essential in grasping the full scope of the Starseed experience. These higher dimensions offer a more expansive view of reality, allowing us to explore aspects of consciousness and existence that remain hidden in our everyday lives. For Starseeds, hyperdimensional travel is a key aspect of their journey, enabling them to fulfill their cosmic mission and aid in the spiritual evolution of humanity. As we continue to explore these realms, we open ourselves to a deeper understanding of the universe and our place within it.

The Nature of Consciousness

In the exploration of hyperdimensional realities and the role of Starseeds, understanding the nature of consciousness is paramount. Consciousness, often regarded as the most profound and elusive phenomenon in the universe, serves as the bridge between the physical world and the higher dimensions of existence. Let's investigate the intricate fabric of consciousness, exploring its definitions, dimensions, and the integral part it plays in the journey of a Starseed.

Defining Consciousness

Consciousness has been a subject of debate and contemplation throughout human history, spanning fields from philosophy and psychology to neuroscience and quantum physics. In its broadest sense, consciousness can be defined as the state of being aware of and able to perceive external and internal experiences. It encompasses a spectrum of experiences, including sensory perception, self-awareness, cognition, and the subjective quality of experience known as qualia.

However, this definition barely scratches the surface of the complexity and depth of consciousness. In many spiritual and metaphysical traditions, consciousness is seen as the fundamental fabric of the universe, a unified field that transcends time and space, from which all physical reality emerges.

Consciousness in Hyperdimensional Context

In the context of hyperdimensional existence, consciousness is not limited to the physical brain or the body. It is instead viewed as a non-local field that permeates and interconnects all aspects of the universe. This perspective aligns with some interpretations of quantum mechanics, where the observer (consciousness) plays a vital role in shaping reality.

For Starseeds, consciousness is the vehicle through which they navigate different dimensions. It allows them to access higher states of awareness, connect with other entities and consciousnesses within these dimensions, and bring back knowledge and insights to their Earthly existence. This expanded view of consciousness is key to understanding how Starseeds perceive and interact with the multiple layers of reality.

Multidimensionality of Consciousness

Consciousness is inherently multidimensional. It exists on a continuum, from the most basic level of physical awareness to the highest planes of cosmic consciousness. These different levels or layers of consciousness correspond to the various dimensions discussed in earlier chapters.

At the higher levels of consciousness, one transcends the ego and the illusion of separateness, experiencing a profound sense of oneness with all existence. This state is often described in mystical experiences and is a hallmark of the Starseed's journey. It is in these elevated states of consciousness that the Starseed's mission and purpose become clear, and their ability to act as conduits for higher-dimensional energies is amplified.

Consciousness is a multi-faceted and profound aspect of our existence, playing a crucial role in our understanding of hyperdimensional realities. For Starseeds, it is the essence of their being and the tool through which they fulfill their cosmic mission. By exploring and expanding our consciousness, we open the door to a deeper understanding of ourselves and the universe, paving the way for a journey of transformation and enlightenment.

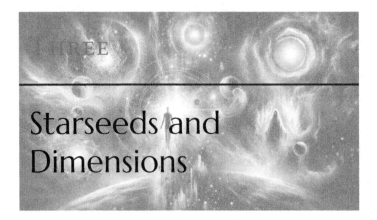

Starseeds and Dimensions

How Starseeds Experience Dimensions

The experience of dimensions by Starseeds is a topic that intertwines the mystical with the tangible, offering a unique perspective on how these beings interact with the multiple layers of reality. Let's explore the multifaceted ways in which Starseeds perceive, engage with, and influence the various dimensions they encounter.

Sensory Perception and Dimensional Awareness

Starseeds often exhibit heightened sensory perception, which extends beyond the five physical senses. Their ability to perceive subtle energies and vibrations allows them to attune to different dimensional frequencies. This heightened awareness can manifest in various forms, such as seeing auras, feeling energy flows, or hearing sounds beyond the normal range of human hearing.

Dimensional awareness for Starseeds is not limited to sensory perception. It also involves a profound intuitive understanding and a deep, often unspoken, knowledge of the interconnectedness of all things across dimensions. This awareness enables them to navigate through dimensions with a sense of purpose and intentionality.

Emotional and Energetic Resonance

Starseeds tend to resonate at a higher emotional and energetic frequency. They are often deeply empathic, feeling the emotions and energies of those around them, sometimes even those from different dimensions. This resonance is not just a passive experience; it actively influences their interactions with the world and the dimensions they traverse.

The emotional and energetic resonance of Starseeds plays a critical role in their mission. It enables them to transmute lower vibrational energies into higher ones, thereby contributing to the healing and elevation of the collective consciousness. Their presence in a specific dimension can bring about significant shifts in the energy dynamics of that realm.

Dimensional Shifting and Manipulation

Starseeds possess an innate ability to shift between dimensions, sometimes consciously and at other times spontaneously. This shifting is not always physical; it often occurs in the realm of consciousness, allowing them to access information, wisdom, and insights from various dimensional planes.

In addition to shifting between dimensions, Starseeds can also manipulate dimensional energies. This manipulation can be for healing, manifesting, teaching, or guiding purposes. They often use this ability to bring about positive changes, whether in the physical realm or in higher dimensions.

Challenges in Dimensional Experiences

While the ability to experience and interact with multiple dimensions is a profound gift, it also comes with its challenges. Starseeds may sometimes feel overwhelmed by the intensity of their experiences or find it difficult to ground themselves in the physical dimension. Navigating the human experience while maintaining a connection to higher dimensions requires a delicate balance and often a period of adjustment and learning.

The way Starseeds experience dimensions is a complex interplay of sensory perception, emotional resonance, and energetic manipulation. Their heightened awareness and abilities allow them to interact with the various layers of reality in ways that are not typically accessible to others. Understanding these experiences is key to comprehending the role of Starseeds in the cosmic tapestry and the impact they have on the evolution of consciousness across dimensions.

Hyperdimensional DNA: Unlocking Your Cosmic Code

The concept of Hyperdimensional DNA transcends the traditional understanding of genetics, exploring the deeper, esoteric aspects of our genetic makeup that connect us with the cosmos. Let's delve into the idea that our DNA holds keys not just to our physical traits but also to our spiritual and multidimensional capabilities, particularly in the context of Starseeds.

Understanding Hyperdimensional DNA

Hyperdimensional DNA refers to the ethereal aspect of our genetic code, which extends beyond the physical double helix into the realm of higher dimensions. It is believed that this multidimensional aspect of our DNA is what connects us to the broader universe, serving as a bridge between our physical form and our cosmic origins.

For Starseeds, the concept of Hyperdimensional DNA is especially significant. It is thought that Starseeds have unique markers or codes within their DNA that resonate with the frequencies of their star origins. These markers are not just physical but are also energetic imprints that carry the wisdom, knowledge, and abilities from these higher dimensional realms.

Activation of Hyperdimensional DNA

The activation of Hyperdimensional DNA is a key process in the awakening journey of a Starseed. This activation is often described as a spiritual awakening, where dormant parts of the DNA are awakened, triggering a profound transformation in consciousness and abilities.

This process can be spontaneous or induced through various spiritual practices such as meditation, energy work, or encounters with higher-dimensional beings. The activation often leads to an expansion of consciousness, enhanced psychic abilities, deeper understanding of one's cosmic mission, and a greater alignment with one's higher self.

The Role of Hyperdimensional DNA in Dimensional Travel

Hyperdimensional DNA plays a crucial role in a Starseed's ability to navigate through different dimensions. It acts as a cosmic GPS, guiding them through the intricacies of the multidimensional universe. With activated Hyperdimensional DNA, Starseeds can attune to the frequencies of various dimensions, enabling them to travel and operate within these realms more effectively.

This DNA also aids in the protection and adaptation of Starseeds as they journey through different energetic environments. It helps in aligning their vibrational frequency with that of the dimension they are interacting with, ensuring their energetic integrity and facilitating their mission.

The Evolutionary Aspect of Hyperdimensional DNA

The concept of Hyperdimensional DNA also carries implications for the evolution of humanity. As more individuals awaken and activate these aspects of their DNA, it is believed that humanity as a whole will undergo a collective shift in consciousness. This shift could lead to a greater understanding of our place in the cosmos, enhanced abilities to interact with higher dimensions, and a deeper connection with the universal consciousness.

Hyperdimensional DNA is a profound and integral part of the Starseed's journey. It is the genetic and energetic link that connects them to the cosmos, enabling them to fulfill their missions. The exploration and understanding of this concept not only provide insights into the nature of Starseeds but also offer a glimpse into the potential evolutionary trajectory of human consciousness.

Multi-Dimensional Self: Unfolding Your Petals

The concept of a Multi-Dimensional Self is central to the understanding of Starseeds and their unique journey through various realms of existence. Let's dive into the layers and complexities of the Multi-Dimensional Self, exploring how Starseeds unfold their potential and navigate their many facets across different dimensions.

Exploring the Layers of the Multi-Dimensional Self

The Multi-Dimensional Self can be envisioned as a spectrum of selves, each existing in different dimensions and vibrational frequencies. These selves range from the physical and emotional to the mental, spiritual, and beyond. For Starseeds, awareness of these different selves is often more pronounced, allowing them to experience a richer tapestry of existence.

This concept extends beyond the traditional understanding of self in three-dimensional terms. It includes higher aspects of being, such as the Higher Self, which represents the most enlightened part of one's consciousness, existing in a higher dimensional space. The Multi-Dimensional Self is in a constant state of flux and evolution, influenced by experiences across various realms and the continuous process of spiritual growth.

Unfolding the Petals of the Multi-Dimensional Self

The journey of a Starseed often involves the unfolding or awakening of these various selves. This process is akin to a flower blooming, where each petal opens up to reveal a new aspect of their being. The unfolding can be gradual or rapid, depending on the individual's life path, experiences, and conscious efforts towards self-realization.

As Starseeds become more attuned to their Multi-Dimensional Self, they gain access to a broader range of abilities, insights, and perspectives. They may experience profound spiritual awakenings, psychic abilities, deep empathic connections, or even recall past life experiences. Each of these aspects offers a piece of the puzzle in understanding their true nature and purpose.

Navigating the Complexities of a Multi-Dimensional Existence

Living as a Multi-Dimensional being comes with its complexities and challenges. Starseeds often find themselves navigating a delicate balance between their earthly lives and their higher-dimensional realities. They may feel out of place in the mundane aspects of life or struggle with the density of the physical world.

Moreover, the awareness of multiple dimensions of existence can sometimes be overwhelming or disorienting. Starseeds may experience phases of intense energy shifts, emotional upheavals, or profound existential questions as they align with their higher selves and integrate their experiences from various dimensions.

Embracing the Wholeness of Being

Ultimately, the path of the Starseed is about embracing the wholeness of their being across all dimensions. It is a journey towards unity and integration, where the different aspects of self-come together in harmony and purpose. This integration is crucial for Starseeds to fulfill their missions and contribute to the collective evolution of consciousness.

The concept of the Multi-Dimensional Self offers a framework for understanding the complex nature of Starseeds and their experiences across different realms of existence. By unfolding the various layers of their being, Starseeds navigate a path of spiritual growth, self-discovery, and cosmic alignment, contributing to their personal evolution and the higher vibrational frequencies of the universe.

Higher Selves and Oversouls

In the realm of hyperdimensional existence, the concepts of Higher Selves and Oversouls are pivotal in understanding the expansive nature of Starseeds. These concepts provide insight into the intricate layers of consciousness and the interconnectedness of various aspects of the self across multiple dimensions. So let's explore these profound elements of hyperdimensional consciousness, illuminating their roles in the journey of Starseeds.

The Higher Self: Gateway to Expanded Consciousness

The Higher Self can be viewed as an individual's ultimate form of consciousness, existing in a higher dimensional reality. It is the most enlightened version of oneself, unbound by the limitations and distortions of the physical world. For Starseeds, the Higher Self is not only a guide and mentor but also a gateway to their multidimensional nature.

This aspect of the self is characterized by an all-encompassing wisdom, unconditional love, and a deep connection to the

Source or universal consciousness. It transcends the ego and the lower self, which is often entangled in the earthly dramas and challenges. The Higher Self remains in constant communication with the earthly aspect, offering guidance, insight, and a broader perspective on life's experiences.

The Oversoul: The Collective Higher Consciousness

While the Higher Self pertains to the individual, the Oversoul represents a collective level of consciousness. It can be thought of as a spiritual repository of multiple Higher Selves, each linked to different incarnations across time and space. The Oversoul encompasses the collective experiences, knowledge, and spiritual evolution of these incarnations, serving as a grand, multidimensional consciousness.

For Starseeds, the Oversoul is particularly significant as it connects them to other aspects of their soul's journey, not just in this lifetime but across many. It provides a sense of continuity and purpose that transcends individual lifetimes, offering a cosmic perspective on their mission and experiences.

Integrating Higher Self and Oversoul Wisdom

One of the key challenges for Starseeds is to integrate the wisdom and guidance of their Higher Self and Oversoul into their earthly existence. This integration involves a harmonization of the physical and spiritual aspects of their being, allowing them to live their earthly life with a heightened sense of purpose and awareness.

Meditation, contemplative practices, and various forms of energy work can facilitate this integration, enabling Starseeds to access and embody the higher vibrational frequencies of their Higher Selves and Oversouls. As they align more closely with these aspects, Starseeds can navigate their earthly challenges with greater ease, bringing their unique gifts and perspectives to the world.

The Role in Cosmic Evolution

The concept of Higher Selves and Oversouls extends beyond individual growth and enlightenment. It plays a crucial role in the collective evolution of consciousness. As Starseeds integrate the wisdom of these higher aspects, they contribute to the elevation of the collective consciousness, aiding in the spiritual awakening and evolution of humanity.

The Higher Self and Oversoul are key components in the hyperdimensional framework of existence. They represent the multi-layered and interconnected nature of consciousness, guiding Starseeds in their journey across dimensions. By embracing and integrating these aspects, Starseeds fulfill their roles as catalysts for spiritual growth and cosmic evolution, weaving their unique thread into the tapestry of the universal consciousness.

Journeys through the Inner Realms

The journey through the inner realms is an integral part of the Starseed's experience, offering profound insights into their own nature and the nature of the universe. These journeys are not just metaphorical but are often literal experiences that take place in the realms of consciousness and higher dimensions. Let's investigate the nature of these journeys, their significance, and the transformative impact they have on Starseeds.

Understanding the Inner Realms

The inner realms refer to the vast, often unexplored landscapes within our consciousness. They encompass everything from the depths of the subconscious mind to the exalted planes of higher dimensional existence. For Starseeds, these realms are familiar territories that they navigate to gain wisdom, healing, and spiritual growth.

These journeys are characterized by vivid experiences that transcend ordinary reality. They may involve encounters with spiritual beings, travel through astral planes, or profound revelations about the nature of existence. Each journey is unique and tailored to the individual's needs and spiritual path.

The Purpose of Inner Realm Journeys

The primary purpose of these journeys is the expansion of consciousness and the evolution of the soul. Starseeds embark on these journeys to:

Heal and Integrate Past Traumas: By revisiting past experiences, whether from this lifetime or previous ones, Starseeds can release old wounds and integrate these lessons into their current existence.

Access Higher Wisdom and Knowledge: The inner realms are rich with spiritual wisdom and knowledge that can guide

Starseeds in their earthly mission. This wisdom often comes in the form of direct teachings from higher-dimensional beings or intuitive insights.

Enhance Their Abilities: Through these journeys, Starseeds often unlock latent abilities such as heightened intuition, psychic powers, or energy healing capabilities.

Techniques for Journeying

Journeys through the inner realms can be initiated through various techniques. These include:

- **Meditation and Visualization**: Deep meditative states can serve as gateways to the inner realms. Visualization techniques can help Starseeds navigate these landscapes with intention.

- **Shamanic Practices**: Traditional shamanic practices, such as drumming, chanting, or plant medicine, can facilitate profound journeys into the inner realms.

- **Dream Work**: Lucid dreaming or dream interpretation can provide valuable insights from the subconscious and higher-dimensional aspects of the self.

Navigating Challenges

Journeying through the inner realms is not without its challenges. Starseeds may encounter confusing or frightening experiences that test their resolve and understanding. Navigating these experiences requires a grounded sense of self, a strong connection to their Higher Self, and the guidance of spiritual mentors or guides.

Moreover, integrating the insights and transformations from these journeys into daily life is crucial. It involves balancing the spiritual and mundane aspects of existence, ensuring that the wisdom gained is applied in a practical and grounded manner.

The Transformative Impact

The transformative impact of these journeys cannot be overstated. Starseeds often emerge with a renewed sense of purpose, deeper self-awareness, and an expanded sense of connectedness to all beings. These journeys catalyze significant spiritual growth, aligning Starseeds more closely with their cosmic mission and facilitating their role as agents of consciousness evolution.

Journeys through the inner realms are a vital aspect of the Starseed's path, offering profound opportunities for healing, growth, and the acquisition of wisdom. These experiences deepen their connection to the universe and their understanding of the intricate tapestry of existence, empowering them to fulfill their destiny as multidimensional beings.

Four
Tools for Hyperdimensional Travel

The Role of Sacred Geometry

Sacred geometry is a fundamental aspect of the universe, acting as the blueprint upon which the cosmos is constructed. For Starseeds and those navigating multiple realities, understanding and utilizing sacred geometry is key to deepening their connection with the multidimensional universe. So let's explore the essence of sacred geometry, its significance in hyperdimensional travel, and practical ways in which it can be used.

Understanding Sacred Geometry

Sacred geometry refers to the patterns, shapes, and forms that are foundational to the existence of all things. These geometrical codes underlie the very fabric of our physical and non-physical reality, from the smallest atomic structures to the vast patterns of the cosmos. Recognized in various spiritual and ancient wisdom traditions, sacred geometry is seen as the visual expression of the harmony and unity inherent in the universe.

At its core, sacred geometry is about understanding the interconnectedness of all things. It reveals how the universe organizes itself, following specific geometric principles that resonate with harmony, balance, and proportion.

Sacred Geometry in Hyperdimensional Travel

For Starseeds, sacred geometry serves as a navigational tool in their journey across dimensions. It provides a harmonic resonance that aligns with the frequencies of different dimensions, facilitating smoother transitions and deeper understanding of these realms.

Gateway to Higher Dimensions: Certain geometric shapes, like the Merkaba or the Flower of Life, are believed to act as vehicles or portals to higher dimensions. They can be used in meditation or visualization practices to access these realms.

Alignment with Cosmic Frequencies: Utilizing sacred geometry helps in aligning one's energy with the cosmic frequencies, aiding in attunement with the universal flow of energy and information.

Enhancing Intuitive and Psychic Abilities: Engaging with sacred geometry can activate and enhance psychic and intuitive abilities, which are essential in perceiving and navigating the hyperdimensional realities.

Practical Applications of Sacred Geometry

Starseeds can incorporate sacred geometry into various aspects of their lives to enhance their connection with the multidimensional universe:

- **Meditation and Visualization**: Using sacred geometric forms as focal points during meditation can facilitate deeper spiritual experiences and connections with higher consciousness.

- **Energy Healing**: Implementing sacred geometry in energy healing practices can enhance the healing process, bringing harmony and balance to the energy fields.

- **Environment Harmonization**: Creating spaces with

elements of sacred geometry, like in the design of living spaces or gardens, can harmonize the energy of the environment, making it conducive to spiritual practices and peaceful living.

- **Art and Creativity**: Expressing sacred geometry through art can be a powerful way to internalize and understand these cosmic patterns, as well as to transmit their harmonizing energies to others.

Sacred geometry is more than just a series of symbols; it is a language that transcends words, conveying the deepest truths of the universe. For Starseeds, engaging with sacred geometry is a means of harmonizing with the cosmic order, enhancing their journey across dimensions, and deepening their understanding of the interconnectedness of all existence. Through sacred geometry, they can access the wisdom and knowledge inherent in the universe, aiding in their mission of spiritual evolution and cosmic exploration.

Utilizing Crystals for Dimensional Work

Crystals, with their unique vibrational signatures and geometric structures, play a significant role in the practice of hyperdimensional travel and energy work for Starseeds. Their ability to store, amplify, and transmute energies makes them valuable tools for navigating and interacting with multiple dimensions. Let's delve into the use of crystals in dimensional work, offering insights into how they can enhance the Starseed's journey.

The Vibrational Power of Crystals

Crystals are more than just physical objects; they are repositories of energy and information. Each type of crystal resonates with a specific frequency, making them ideal for aligning with different dimensional energies. This resonance is due to their unique internal structures, which are geometrically aligned in a way that allows them to hold and emit energetic patterns.

For Starseeds, crystals act as anchors and amplifiers for higher dimensional energies. They can be used to create energetic grids, enhance meditative states, and even facilitate communication with higher dimensional beings.

Selecting Crystals for Dimensional Work

Choosing the right crystals is a vital part of effective dimensional work. Different crystals resonate with different dimensions and aspects of the self. For instance:

- **Amethyst** is often used for its connection to the Third Eye and Crown Chakras, enhancing psychic abilities and spiritual awareness.

- **Clear Quartz** is known for its ability to amplify energy and intention, making it a versatile tool for various types of energy work.

- **Rose Quartz** emanates a vibration of unconditional love, aiding in emotional healing and the opening of the Heart Chakra.

- **Black Tourmaline** and **Shungite** are used for grounding and protective energies, especially important when navigating higher dimensions.

Using Crystals in Dimensional Practices

Crystals can be integrated into various practices to enhance the Starseed's connection with different dimensions:

Meditation and Visualization: Holding or placing crystals on specific energy centers (chakras) during meditation can deepen the experience and facilitate a clearer connection with higher dimensions.

Energy Grids: Creating geometric patterns with crystals can help in anchoring energies from higher dimensions into the physical realm, creating spaces of high vibrational frequency.

Healing Work: Using crystals in energy healing can help in balancing the chakras, releasing blockages, and harmonizing the physical and subtle bodies.

Cleansing and Programming Crystals

To maximize their effectiveness, crystals need to be regularly cleansed and programmed with intention. Cleansing can be done using methods such as smudging, burying in the earth, or using running water. Programming involves setting specific intentions or connecting the crystal with particular dimensional energies, which can be done through meditation and visualization.

Ethical Considerations

It's important to source crystals ethically, respecting the Earth and the regions from which they are mined. Understanding the origin of crystals and the conditions under which they were obtained adds to the energetic integrity of the work done with them.

Crystals are powerful allies for Starseeds engaging in hyperdimensional work. Their vibrational qualities and geometric structures make them ideal for connecting with, navigating, and working within multiple dimensions. By selecting, cleansing, and programming crystals with intention, Starseeds can significantly enhance their dimensional practices, deepen their spiritual journey, and contribute to their mission of raising the collective consciousness.

Advanced Meditation Techniques

Meditation is a key practice for Starseeds in navigating multiple realities. It serves as a gateway to higher dimensions, a tool for inner transformation, and a method for attaining deeper understanding of the self and the universe. So let's take a deep dive into advanced meditation techniques that facilitate these multidimensional journeys, offering Starseeds and others pathways to profound spiritual experiences.

Deepening the Meditative State

To access higher dimensions and connect with their multi-dimensional selves, Starseeds must go beyond basic meditation practices. Deepening the meditative state involves techniques that transcend ordinary consciousness and open doorways to other realms of existence.

Trance Meditation: This involves entering a trance-like state where the practitioner becomes deeply absorbed in the meditative experience, often losing awareness of the physical body. This state can facilitate astral travel, profound visionary experiences, and deep insights.

Chakra Meditation: Focusing intensely on the chakras (energy centers within the body) can unlock higher states of consciousness. Each chakra corresponds to different aspects of our being and, when activated, can open new levels of awareness and capabilities.

Mantra Meditation: The use of sacred sounds or mantras can elevate the mind to higher vibrational states. These sounds resonate with specific frequencies and can help align the practitioner's energy with higher dimensional realities.

Techniques for Dimensional Exploration

For Starseeds wishing to explore different dimensions, certain meditation techniques can be particularly effective:

- **Guided Visualization**: This involves following a guided journey, often led by a teacher or a recording, which takes the practitioner through various landscapes and scenarios. These visualizations can be gateways to other dimensions and realities.

- **Third Eye Meditation**: Focusing on the area between the eyebrows, believed to be the seat of the third eye, can facilitate psychic opening and clairvoyant experiences. This practice can lead to seeing into other dimensions or receiving intuitive knowledge.

- **Breathwork and Energy Flow**: Controlled breathing techniques, combined with the visualization of energy flow, can raise the practitioner's vibrational frequency, making it easier to access higher dimensions.

Integrating Meditation Experiences

Experiences in higher dimensions can be intense and transformative. Integrating these experiences into one's daily life is crucial for the Starseed's growth and effectiveness in their mission. This involves:

- **Reflection and Journaling**: Documenting and reflecting upon the meditative experiences helps in understanding and integrating the insights and lessons learned.

- **Grounding Practices**: After deep meditative journeys, grounding exercises such as walking in nature, eating nourishing foods, or engaging in physical activity can help in re-establishing the connection with the physical world.

- **Sharing and Community**: Engaging with a community of like-minded individuals can provide support and a space for sharing experiences and insights.

Ethical Considerations

With great power comes great responsibility. Starseeds must approach these practices with respect, understanding the potential impact of their explorations both on themselves and the wider universe. Ethical considerations include respecting the integrity of other beings and dimensions encountered and using the insights gained for positive transformation.

Advanced meditation techniques offer Starseeds powerful tools for exploring multiple dimensions, gaining profound wisdom, and fulfilling their cosmic roles. By deepening their meditative practices, Starseeds can navigate the complexities of their multi-dimensional existence, contributing to their personal evolution and the collective advancement of consciousness.

Developing Your Third Eye

The Third Eye, also known as the Ajna Chakra in Eastern traditions, is a pivotal energy center for Starseeds and those engaged in multidimensional work. It is often considered the gateway to higher consciousness, intuition, and psychic abilities. Let's explore the significance of the Third Eye in hyperdimensional experiences and offers practices to develop and enhance its capabilities.

Understanding the Third Eye

The Third Eye is located in the center of the forehead, just above the space between the eyebrows. It is associated with the pineal gland, a small endocrine gland in the brain known for producing melatonin, a hormone that regulates sleep patterns. In metaphysical terms, the Third Eye is the seat of intuition, insight, and spiritual vision. It allows individuals to perceive beyond the physical, into the realms of subtle energies and higher dimensions.

Awakening the Third Eye

Awakening the Third Eye is a transformative process that enables deeper understanding and perception of the non-physical realms. This awakening can be cultivated through various practices:

- **Meditation**: Focused meditation on the Third Eye can stimulate this energy center, enhancing clairvoyant abilities and spiritual insight. Visualization techniques, such as picturing an indigo light or an eye opening in the forehead, can be particularly effective.

- **Breathing Exercises**: Specific pranayama techniques,

like alternate nostril breathing, can balance and activate the Third Eye. These practices help in harmonizing the left and right hemispheres of the brain, which is essential for opening this chakra.

- **Diet and Lifestyle**: A balanced diet, rich in organic and natural foods, can support the health of the pineal gland. Avoiding fluoride and using detoxifying practices can also be beneficial, as fluoride is believed to calcify the pineal gland and inhibit its function.

Practices to Enhance Third Eye Abilities

Once the Third Eye begins to awaken, certain practices can enhance its abilities:

- **Crystal Therapy**: Crystals such as amethyst, lapis lazuli, and sapphire can be used to stimulate and balance the Third Eye. Placing these crystals on the forehead during meditation can enhance psychic abilities.

- **Chanting and Sound Therapy**: The sound 'OM' or 'AUM' is traditionally associated with the Third Eye. Chanting this mantra can resonate with and activate this energy center.

- **Sun Gazing**: Practicing sun gazing during safe hours (dawn or dusk) can stimulate the pineal gland. However, this should be done cautiously and with proper guidance.

Challenges and Cautions

While developing the Third Eye can lead to profound spiritual experiences, it also comes with responsibilities and potential challenges. Overstimulation can lead to confusion, psychic overwhelm, or detachment from the physical world. It's crucial to approach these practices with balance and grounding techniques, ensuring that both spiritual and earthly responsibilities are maintained.

Ethical Considerations

With increased psychic abilities, ethical considerations become paramount. It's important to use these gifts with respect, compassion, and for the highest good of all. Developing the Third Eye should go hand in hand with the development of wisdom, empathy, and understanding.

The Third Eye is a powerful tool for Starseeds and those exploring hyperdimensional realities. Its development enhances psychic abilities, deepens spiritual understanding, and allows for a more profound connection with the universe. Approaching this practice with balance, respect, and a grounded sense of responsibility ensures that its gifts are used wisely and effectively.

Astral Projection and Remote Viewing

Astral projection and remote viewing are advanced techniques often utilized by Starseeds for exploring multidimensional realities and gathering information from afar. These practices allow for consciousness to travel beyond the physical body, providing unique perspectives and profound insights. This chapter delves into the nature of astral projection and remote viewing, their significance for Starseeds, and methods to safely practice these techniques.

Understanding Astral Projection

Astral projection, also known as astral travel, is the practice of consciously directing one's astral body or consciousness to travel outside the physical body to various destinations. This experience often involves visiting different dimensions, planes of existence, or distant locations on Earth. During astral projection, individuals may encounter various entities, landscapes, and phenomena that are not accessible in the physical realm.

Techniques for Astral Projection

Relaxation and Visualization: The key to successful astral projection lies in deep relaxation and the use of visualization techniques. Practitioners often start by visualizing themselves floating away from their physical body or imagining a rope that they can climb to pull themselves out of their physical form.

Energy Work: Energy manipulation techniques, such as working with the chakras or visualizing energy flowing through the body, can help in loosening the astral body from the physical one.

Mindfulness and Focus: Maintaining a state of mindfulness and focused intent is crucial for controlling the experience and ensuring a purposeful journey.

Remote Viewing: An Overview

Remote viewing is a practice where individuals use their psychic ability to see or perceive a distant location or event that is not within their physical sight. Unlike astral projection, remote viewing does not involve leaving the body but rather extending one's perceptual abilities across space and time.

Applications and Techniques of Remote Viewing

Information Gathering: Remote viewing can be used for gathering information about distant places, people, or events, both in the present and, at times, in the past or potential future.

Structured Approach: Remote viewing often follows a more structured approach compared to astral projection, involving specific protocols and stages designed to enhance accuracy and clarity of perception.

Practice and Development: Regular practice, often under controlled conditions, is necessary to develop and refine remote viewing skills. This may include exercises to enhance focus, concentration, and visualization abilities.

Safety and Ethical Considerations

Both astral projection and remote viewing should be approached with caution and respect for one's own boundaries and the privacy of others. Practitioners must:

- **Ensure Protection**: Employing spiritual protection techniques is crucial to safeguard against negative entities or energies encountered during astral travels.

- **Respect Privacy**: Ethical considerations are paramount, especially in remote viewing, as it involves accessing information about others or distant places.

- **Grounding and Integration**: After practicing these techniques, grounding exercises are essential to reintegrate the consciousness with the physical body and reality.

Significance for Starseeds

For Starseeds, astral projection and remote viewing are not merely tools for exploration but are integral to their mission. These practices allow them to gather knowledge, connect with other entities or dimensions, and perform tasks that contribute to their overarching objectives of spiritual growth, healing, and cosmic understanding.

Astral projection and remote viewing are profound practices that offer Starseeds and others access to the vastness of the universe beyond the physical constraints. With proper training, ethical considerations, and a clear intention, these techniques can unlock new levels of awareness and facilitate the fulfillment of one's higher purpose.

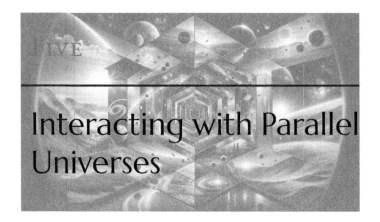

Interacting with Parallel Universes

Starseeds and The Mandela Effect

The Mandela Effect, a phenomenon where a large group of people remember an event or detail differently than how it is recorded in history or reality, presents a fascinating intersection with the experiences of Starseeds. Let's explore the connection between Starseeds and the Mandela Effect, offering insights into how this phenomenon might be understood within the context of multidimensional realities.

Understanding the Mandela Effect

The Mandela Effect refers to collective misremembering of specific facts or events. Named after the widespread false memory of Nelson Mandela dying in prison in the 1980s (he actually passed away in 2013), this phenomenon includes a variety of instances where public recollection diverges from recorded history. This has led to numerous theories, ranging from psychological explanations to the idea of parallel universes and alternate realities.

Starseeds and Dimensional Shifts

For Starseeds, the Mandela Effect may be more than just a curious anomaly. It could be indicative of their sensitivity to shifts in dimensional realities. Starseeds, often attuned to higher frequencies and possessing a deep connection with the cosmos, might be more likely to notice discrepancies caused by shifts in timelines or realities.

Alternate Histories and Timelines: Some theories suggest that the Mandela Effect is a result of changes in timelines or shifts between parallel universes. Starseeds, with their heightened awareness, might be more attuned to these changes, noticing discrepancies that others overlook.

Collective Consciousness Influence: Another perspective is that the Mandela Effect results from collective consciousness influencing reality. As Starseeds often work towards elevating collective consciousness, they might be more sensitive to its fluctuations and effects.

Implications for Multidimensional Existence

The Mandela Effect has intriguing implications for the concept of a multidimensional universe, a core aspect of Starseed philosophy:

- **Evidence of Multidimensionality**: For those who believe in multiple dimensions, the Mandela Effect might be seen as evidence of this complex reality structure, where different dimensions or realities can overlap or intersect.

- **Navigating Multiple Realities**: Understanding the Mandela Effect can be crucial for Starseeds in their mission. It underscores the importance of awareness and adaptability in navigating a universe where reality is not always a fixed, unchanging construct.

Coping with Reality Shifts

For Starseeds who experience the Mandela Effect, coping with these shifts in reality can be challenging:

- **Maintaining Balance**: Staying grounded and maintaining a balance between different perceptions of reality is crucial. This involves integrating their experiences into a cohesive understanding of the world and their purpose in it.

- **Sharing Experiences**: Communicating with other Starseeds or like-minded individuals can provide support and validation for experiences related to the Mandela Effect. It can also help in collectively piecing together the puzzle of these phenomena.

The Mandela Effect presents an intriguing aspect of reality that resonates with the experiences of Starseeds. It highlights the potential for shifts in collective memory and reality, echoing the Starseed understanding of a fluid, multidimensional universe. By exploring and acknowledging these experiences, Starseeds can gain deeper insights into the nature of reality and their role in navigating and influencing it.

Time Loops and Temporal Distortions

In the exploration of hyperdimensional realities, the concepts of time loops and temporal distortions present intriguing phenomena for Starseeds. These occurrences challenge the conventional understanding of time, offering insights into the fluid and malleable nature of reality as experienced in multiple dimensions. Let's delve into the nature of time loops and temporal distortions, their significance for Starseeds, and the ways they navigate these complex phenomena.

Understanding Time Loops

Time loops refer to the experience of a period or moment in time repeating itself. This phenomenon, often associated with déjà vu, can range from a fleeting sensation to more prolonged experiences where events seem to replay over a duration. In the context of hyperdimensional existence, time loops may be indicative of:

- **Cyclic Patterns of Learning**: Time loops can represent cycles of learning where certain experiences or lessons repeat until fully understood or integrated.

- **Dimensional Overlaps**: They may also occur when there is an overlap or convergence of different timelines or dimensions, causing a temporal glitch or loop.

Temporal Distortions in Multidimensional Realities

Temporal distortions involve alterations in the perception or experience of time. In multidimensional realities, time is not linear but fluid, leading to phenomena where time may seem to speed up, slow down, or behave unpredictably. These distortions can be experienced during:

- **Deep Meditative States**: In heightened states of consciousness, the perception of time can significantly alter.

- **Astral Travel or Dimensional Journeys**: When navigating different dimensions, Starseeds might experience time differently, as the rules of time can vary across dimensions.

Navigating Time Loops and Temporal Distortions

For Starseeds, understanding and navigating time loops and temporal distortions are crucial for their work and personal growth:

- **Conscious Awareness**: Developing an awareness of these phenomena allows Starseeds to recognize and understand their experiences within time loops or temporal distortions.

- **Learning from Repetitions**: By identifying patterns within time loops, Starseeds can uncover lessons or unresolved issues needing attention, aiding their spiritual and dimensional work.

- **Maintaining Vibrational Integrity**: Staying grounded and maintaining a high vibrational state can help Starseeds navigate temporal distortions without losing touch with their core purpose and mission.

Implications for Cosmic Evolution

Time loops and temporal distortions have profound implications for the evolution of consciousness:

- **Understanding Multidimensionality**: These phenomena highlight the complexity of the universe and the non-linear nature of time, offering a broader perspective of reality.

- **Catalysts for Change**: By experiencing and understanding these temporal anomalies, Starseeds can become catalysts for change, helping to elevate collective consciousness and bring about evolutionary shifts.

Time loops and temporal distortions present both challenges and opportunities for Starseeds. These phenomena provide a deeper understanding of the malleable nature of time and reality in a multidimensional context. By learning to navigate these occurrences, Starseeds can harness their unique insights and experiences to aid in their mission of cosmic evolution and collective awakening.

Understanding Synchronicity

Synchronicity, a concept first introduced by Carl Jung, refers to the meaningful coincidences that occur in our lives, where seemingly unrelated events are connected by meaning rather than cause. For Starseeds navigating multiple realities, synchronicity serves as a guiding force and a language of the universe, revealing deeper patterns and connections. Let's explore the role of synchronicity in the hyperdimensional experience, offering insights into its significance and how to interpret and utilize these meaningful coincidences.

The Nature of Synchronicity

Synchronicity transcends the conventional understanding of time and causality. It operates on the principle that the universe is fundamentally interconnected and that our thoughts, emotions, and intentions can align with external events to convey messages, guidance, or affirmation. These synchronistic events are often experienced as:

- **Coincidences that seem too precise to be mere chance.**
- **Patterns that recur in various forms, such as repeating numbers, symbols, or themes.**
- **Events that directly relate to thoughts, conversations, or needs at the moment they occur.**

Synchronicity as a Dimensional Intersection

For Starseeds, synchronicity is not just an occasional curious phenomenon but a consistent aspect of their journey. It can be seen as:

- **A Signpost of Alignment**: Synchronicities often occur when Starseeds are aligned with their higher purpose or path. They act as affirmations from the universe or their guides.

- **A Tool for Navigation**: In the complex terrain of multiple dimensions, synchronicities serve as navigational aids, helping Starseeds decide on directions or actions.

- **A Method of Communication**: These events can be perceived as messages from higher selves, spiritual guides, or the universal consciousness.

Interpreting Synchronicities

Understanding and interpreting synchronicities requires intuition and attentiveness. Starseeds often develop an acute sense of awareness to discern the meanings behind these events. This process involves:

- **Observation and Reflection**: Noting down synchronistic events and reflecting on their possible meanings or implications.

- **Intuitive Listening**: Tuning into one's intuition to understand the deeper significance of these occurrences.

- **Connecting the Dots**: Looking at the larger picture and understanding how these events relate to the journey and lessons of the Starseed.

Practical Applications

In daily life, synchronicities can be applied in several ways:

- **Guidance in Decision Making**: Synchronistic events can provide clarity or confirmation when making important decisions.

- **Spiritual and Personal Development**: They can highlight areas of growth, unresolved issues, or new paths to explore.

- **Creative Inspiration**: Many artists, writers, and innovators have found inspiration in synchronistic experiences, leading to profound works and ideas.

Challenges and Misinterpretations

While synchronicity is a powerful tool, it also comes with challenges:

- **Over-Interpretation**: There's a risk of reading too much into ordinary events, leading to confusion or misdirection.

- **Balance Between Intuition and Rationality**: Maintaining a balance between intuitive interpretations and rational thinking is crucial to avoid being led astray by false patterns or meanings.

Synchronicity is a significant aspect of the hyperdimensional experience for Starseeds. It serves as a bridge between the multiple layers of reality, providing guidance, affirmation, and insight. By learning to recognize, interpret, and utilize these meaningful coincidences, Starseeds can navigate their journey with greater clarity and purpose, aligning more closely with their missions and the higher flow of the universe.

Manifestation Across Dimensions

Manifestation, the ability to bring into reality one's thoughts, intentions, and desires, takes on a new dimension in the context of hyperdimensional starseeds. These individuals, with their deep connection to multiple layers of existence, engage with manifestation in unique ways that transcend conventional understandings. This chapter delves into the principles of multidimensional manifestation, exploring how starseeds can effectively harness this power to influence their journey and the broader universe.

Multidimensional Manifestation

In the realm of hyperdimensional starseeds, manifestation is not limited to the physical plane. It encompasses the ability to bring forth changes and effects across various dimensions of existence. This involves:

- **Thoughts and Intentions**: Recognizing that thoughts and intentions are powerful energies that can influence reality across dimensions.

- **Vibrational Alignment**: Understanding that aligning one's vibration with desired outcomes is key to manifestation, especially when these outcomes span different realms of existence.

Techniques for Effective Manifestation

Starseeds utilize a range of techniques to manifest across dimensions, including:

Focused Intention: Setting clear, focused intentions is the first step in the manifestation process. This involves not only knowing what one desires but also why and how it aligns with one's higher purpose.

Visualization: Visualization is a powerful tool in manifestation. It involves creating a mental image of the desired outcome, imbuing it with emotions and senses to bring it closer to reality.

Energy Work: Utilizing energy practices like meditation, chakra alignment, or working with crystals can amplify manifestation efforts, aligning internal energies with desired outcomes.

Affirmations and Decrees: Speaking or mentally affirming one's intentions helps solidify them in the conscious and subconscious mind, aiding in their manifestation.

Manifestation and Time

In hyperdimensional contexts, the concept of time plays a crucial role in manifestation:

- **Non-Linear Manifestation**: Starseeds understand that manifestation may not follow a linear timeline. Outcomes can materialize in unexpected ways and times, influenced by the dynamics of different dimensions.

- **Patience and Trust**: Developing patience and trust in the process is vital, as manifestations may unfold over different timelines and in various dimensional realities.

Ethical Considerations

Ethical considerations are paramount in multidimensional manifestation:

- **For the Greater Good**: Starseeds are encouraged to manifest with the intention of benefiting not just themselves but the greater good, considering the impact of their desires on multiple levels of existence.

- **Karmic Consequences**: Being mindful of the karmic impact of one's manifestations is crucial. This involves considering the consequences of one's desires and actions across dimensions.

Challenges in Multidimensional Manifestation

Starseeds may face unique challenges in their manifestation journey:

- **Dimensional Discrepancies**: Managing the discrepancies between different dimensional realities can be challenging, as what is desired in one dimension may not align with another.

- **Maintaining Focus**: With the vastness of their consciousness, maintaining focus on specific intentions can be challenging for starseeds.

Manifestation for hyperdimensional starseeds involves a deep understanding of the interconnectedness of thoughts, intentions, and realities across multiple dimensions. By mastering focused intention, vibrational alignment, and ethical manifestation, starseeds can effectively influence their reality and contribute to the greater cosmic tapestry. This chapter offers insights into the nuances of multidimensional manifestation, providing guidance for starseeds to harness this powerful ability.

Divergent Timelines and Convergence

In the journey of a hyperdimensional starseed, the concept of divergent timelines and their convergence plays a pivotal role. Let's delve into the intricate nature of timelines within the multidimensional universe, exploring how starseeds navigate these divergences and convergences to fulfill their missions and aid in the evolution of consciousness.

Understanding Divergent Timelines

Divergent timelines are alternate pathways that reality can take, branching out based on decisions, events, or changes in consciousness. Each timeline represents a different possibility or reality, and within the multiverse, countless such timelines exist. These divergences are more than mere theoretical possibilities; they are tangible realities in the hyperdimensional space.

- **Creation of Timelines**: Timelines diverge due to various factors, including individual choices, collective decisions, energetic shifts, and cosmic events.
- **Navigating Timelines**: Starseeds, with their en-

hanced perception, are often aware of these divergences and may consciously choose which timeline to follow based on their intuition and guidance from higher dimensions.

The Role of Convergence

Convergence occurs when separate timelines come together, merging into a unified path. This phenomenon is crucial in the context of cosmic evolution and the ascension process. Convergence points are often marked by significant global events, shifts in collective consciousness, or personal awakenings.

- **Harmonizing Timelines**: The process of convergence involves the harmonization of different realities, leading to a more unified and coherent collective experience.

- **Impact on Starseeds**: For starseeds, these convergence points can be intense periods of transformation, offering opportunities for accelerated growth and the fulfillment of their missions.

Navigating the Complexity of Timelines

For starseeds, understanding and navigating the complex web of timelines involves several key aspects:

Intuitive Guidance: Relying on their intuition and inner guidance to navigate through the complexities of divergent timelines.

Energy Work and Meditation: Utilizing energy work and meditation to attune themselves to higher frequencies, enabling clearer perception of timeline dynamics.

Alignment with Higher Purpose: Making choices and taking actions that align with their higher purpose, thus choosing timelines that resonate with their mission.

Challenges and Opportunities

Navigating divergent timelines and convergence points presents both challenges and opportunities for starseeds:

- **Energetic Overload**: The intensity of converging timelines can be overwhelming, requiring starseeds to practice grounding and self-care.

- **Opportunities for Growth**: These periods can accelerate personal and spiritual growth, offering profound insights and opportunities to make significant impacts.

The Greater Cosmic Perspective

In the grand scheme of the multiverse, divergent timelines and their convergence play a crucial role in the evolution of consciousness. They represent the fluid and dynamic nature of reality, offering a playground for souls to experience, grow, and evolve. For starseeds, these phenomena are not only crucial aspects of their journey but also key to their role in aiding the collective evolution of consciousness.

The concept of divergent timelines and convergence is fundamental to the hyperdimensional existence of starseeds. It offers a deeper understanding of the multidimensional nature of reality, providing a framework for navigating the complexities of the multiverse and contributing to the collective journey towards higher consciousness.

Starseeds and Time-Space Reality

Time as a Dimension

In the exploration of hyperdimensional realities, the concept of time transcends its traditional perception as a linear, unidirectional flow. For starseeds, time is not just a measure of moments but a dimension in itself, offering a profound understanding of existence across multiple realities. So let's delve into the nature of time as experienced by starseeds, highlighting its malleability and significance in their multidimensional journey.

Time: Beyond Linear Progression

For starseeds, time is a fluid and dynamic dimension that can expand, contract, and even loop back upon itself. This non-linear approach to time is key to understanding their experiences in various dimensions:

- **Multidimensional Experience**: Time in different dimensions can flow at varying rates, or even in non-linear patterns, creating unique experiences for starseeds traversing these realms.

- **Past, Present, and Future**: In the hyperdimensional perspective, past, present, and future are viewed as interconnected and accessible segments of the time continuum, rather than sequential stages.

Time Dilation and Compression

Starseeds often experience time dilation (slowing down of time) and time compression (speeding up of time), especially during deep meditative states, astral travel, or significant energetic shifts:

- **Altered States of Consciousness**: In heightened states of awareness, starseeds may experience time differently, with moments of insight stretching for what feels like hours, or hours condensing into moments.

- **Navigating Time Shifts**: Understanding and adapting to these shifts in time perception is crucial for starseeds to maintain equilibrium in their multidimensional existence.

Time as a Tool for Healing and Growth

Time's malleability offers starseeds unique opportunities for healing and growth:

- **Healing Across Time**: Starseeds can work with their past selves or future potentials for deep healing and resolution of karmic patterns.

- **Learning from Parallel Timelines**: By accessing different timelines, starseeds can gather wisdom and insights, enhancing their understanding and evolution.

Challenges in Time Navigation

Navigating time as a dimension comes with its challenges:

- **Temporal Disorientation**: Frequent shifts in time perception can lead to a sense of disorientation or detachment from the conventional time-bound world.

- **Balancing Multiple Timelines**: Managing experiences and responsibilities across different timelines requires a high level of consciousness and grounding.

Integrating Time in Daily Life

For starseeds, integrating their understanding of time into daily life enhances their ability to live in harmony with their multidimensional nature:

- **Mindful Presence**: Embracing the fluidity of time encourages a more mindful, present-focused approach to life.

- **Synchronicity and Flow**: Recognizing the synchronistic flow of events can help starseeds align with the natural rhythm of the universe.

The concept of time as a dimension opens up a vast landscape of possibilities for starseeds. By embracing the non-linear, interconnected nature of time, they can navigate their multidimensional reality with greater ease and purpose. Understanding time in this expanded context allows starseeds to explore their full potential, facilitate profound healing, and contribute to the evolution of consciousness across dimensions.

Navigating the Quantum Field

For hyperdimensional starseeds, the quantum field is not just a theoretical construct, but a tangible reality they interact with on their multidimensional journey. Let's explore the complexities of navigating the quantum field, understanding its principles, and harnessing its potential to enhance their journey across dimensions.

Understanding the Quantum Field

The quantum field is an all-encompassing field of energy and potential that underlies and interconnects all of existence. It's where science and spirituality converge, offering a framework for understanding the deeper mechanics of the universe.

- **The Nature of the Field**: The quantum field is composed of subatomic particles and waves, existing in a state of potential until observed or interacted with.

- **Quantum Entanglement**: This principle posits that particles can be interconnected in such a way that the state of one instantly influences the state of another, regardless of distance, reflecting a deep interconnectedness of all things.

Navigating the Quantum Field

Starseeds, with their heightened awareness, are uniquely positioned to navigate and interact with the quantum field:

- **Conscious Interaction**: By focusing their intention and consciousness, starseeds can interact with the quantum field to bring about changes in their reality and across dimensions.

- **Manifestation and Creation**: Understanding the principles of the quantum field enables starseeds to manifest and create more effectively, as they align with the fundamental energies of the universe.

Tools for Quantum Navigation

Several tools and practices can assist starseeds in navigating the quantum field:

Meditation and Visualization: These practices help in attuning to the quantum field, allowing starseeds to sense and influence the web of energies.

Energy Work: Techniques such as Reiki, Qi Gong, and other forms of energy manipulation can help in interacting with the quantum field.

Sacred Geometry: Understanding the patterns and structures within the quantum field, as revealed through sacred geometry, can provide deeper insights into its workings.

Challenges in Quantum Navigation

While navigating the quantum field offers immense potential, it also comes with challenges:

- **Complexity of the Field**: The quantum field is immensely complex, and understanding its nuances requires deep study and intuition.

- **Responsibility**: With the power to influence reality comes the responsibility to use it wisely, ensuring actions are aligned with higher purposes and the greater good.

Ethical Considerations

Ethical considerations are paramount in quantum navigation:

- **Respecting Free Will**: It's essential to respect the free will and journey of others, avoiding manipulation or interference.

- **Alignment with Universal Laws**: Actions taken within the quantum field should be in harmony with universal laws and principles, such as the Law of One and the Principle of Correspondence.

Navigating the quantum field is a profound aspect of the hyperdimensional starseed's journey. It requires a deep understanding of the interconnectedness of all things, a responsible and ethical approach, and a commitment to using this knowledge for the greater good. By mastering the art of quantum navigation, starseeds can significantly advance their spiritual evolution and contribute to the collective evolution of consciousness.

Theories of Everything: Unified Field Theory

In the exploration of hyperdimensional realities, the quest for a Unified Field Theory (UFT) takes on a profound significance. This theory, a holy grail of sorts in both physics and metaphysics, seeks to explain all fundamental forces and particles in the universe within a single framework. Let's investigate the concept of UFT from a hyperdimensional starseed perspective, examining its implications for understanding the cosmos and their place within it.

The Quest for Unification

The pursuit of a Unified Field Theory is not just a scientific endeavor but also a deeply spiritual one for starseeds. It represents the harmonizing of all universal laws and forces:

- **Integration of Forces**: UFT aims to integrate the four fundamental forces of nature - gravity, electromagnetism, the strong nuclear force, and the weak nuclear force.

- **Beyond Standard Physics**: While contemporary physics offers the Standard Model of particle physics, UFT extends beyond this, positing a more comprehensive understanding of the universe.

Hyperdimensional Implications

For starseeds, the implications of UFT go beyond mere scientific curiosity; they touch the core of their multidimensional experience:

- **Understanding Multidimensionality**: A complete Unified Field Theory would provide a framework for understanding how different dimensions interact and coexist.

- **Consciousness and the Cosmos**: UFT offers a way to understand consciousness not as a byproduct of the brain but as an integral part of the cosmic fabric.

Starseeds and the UFT

Starseeds, with their unique perspectives and experiences, contribute to the evolving understanding of UFT:

- **Experiential Insights**: Starseeds often have experiences that challenge conventional scientific understanding, offering anecdotal evidence and insights that could contribute to the development of UFT.

- **Bridging Science and Spirituality**: Starseeds are

uniquely positioned to bridge the gap between science and spirituality, two fields that UFT inherently unifies.

Challenges in Formulating UFT

The journey towards a Unified Field Theory is fraught with challenges:

- **Complexity of the Universe**: The sheer complexity and scale of the universe make it a daunting task to formulate a theory that explains everything.

- **Integration of Disparate Fields**: Merging theories from different branches of physics, such as quantum mechanics and general relativity, is a significant hurdle.

Ethical and Philosophical Considerations

The pursuit of UFT raises several ethical and philosophical questions:

- **Impact on Humanity's Worldview**: How would a complete understanding of the universe change humanity's perspective on life, purpose, and existence?

- **Responsibility of Knowledge**: With greater understanding comes greater responsibility – how should this knowledge be used for the benefit of all beings?

The Unified Field Theory represents not just a scientific milestone but a transformative philosophical and spiritual revelation, especially for hyperdimensional starseeds. It holds the promise of unraveling the mysteries of the universe, offering a deeper understanding of the intricate tapestry of existence in which they play an integral part. As starseeds and scientists alike continue to explore and expand upon this theory, the potential for profound shifts in our understanding of reality looms ever closer.

Dealing with Time Dilation

Time dilation, a concept rooted in the realms of physics and the extraordinary experiences of starseeds, refers to the difference in elapsed time measured by two observers, owing to a relative velocity between them or a difference in gravitational potential. Let's delve into the nuances of time dilation, particularly from the viewpoint of starseeds navigating multiple realities.

Understanding Time Dilation

To comprehend time dilation, one must venture beyond conventional notions of linear time:

- **Relativity and Time**: Einstein's theory of relativity posits that time is not a constant, but rather varies depending on speed and gravity. This concept is central to understanding the varying experiences of time in different dimensions.

- **Experiencing Different Realities**: Starseeds often report altered perceptions of time, which can be linked to their experiences in various dimensional states.

Time Dilation in Multidimensional Travel

Time dilation becomes particularly pertinent when considering the experiences of starseeds who journey across dimensions:

- **Varied Time Flows**: In different dimensions, the flow of time can vary significantly, a phenomenon often experienced by starseeds during astral travel or deep meditative states.

- **Challenges in Syncing Timelines**: Navigating through dimensions can lead to challenges in aligning with the Earth's time, leading to experiences of time loss or expansion.

Coping Strategies for Starseeds

Managing the effects of time dilation is crucial for starseeds to maintain equilibrium between their multidimensional experiences and earthly existence:

- **Grounding Techniques**: Practices like meditation, connecting with nature, and grounding exercises help starseeds realign with Earth's temporal flow.
- **Temporal Awareness**: Developing a heightened awareness of time's fluidity and practicing mindful presence can assist starseeds in better navigating temporal shifts.

Time Dilation's Impact on Consciousness

Time dilation does not merely alter one's perception of time; it also profoundly affects consciousness:

- **Expanded Consciousness**: Experiencing different flows of time can lead to an expansion of consciousness, allowing starseeds to perceive reality beyond the linear constraints of time.

- **Integration of Experiences**: Balancing these expanded perceptions with day-to-day life is essential for the holistic growth and well-being of a starseed.

Time dilation is a complex yet fascinating aspect of hyperdimensional existence that starseeds frequently encounter. By understanding and embracing the fluidity of time, starseeds can navigate their multidimensional journeys with greater ease and clarity. This knowledge not only aids in their personal evolution but also enhances their ability to contribute positively to the collective consciousness. As we continue to explore the mysteries of the universe, the phenomenon of time dilation offers a unique perspective on the interconnectedness of all existence and the boundless potential of consciousness.

Temporal Mechanics in Daily Life

Let's take a look at the integration of temporal mechanics within the daily lives of hyperdimensional starseeds. This integration is crucial for balancing their multidimensional experiences with the practicalities of earthly existence. Temporal mechanics, in this context, refers to the understanding and application of time's fluid nature in everyday life.

Integrating Multidimensional Time Awareness

The perception of time for a starseed is often non-linear, influenced by their experiences across various dimensions. Incorporating this understanding into daily life involves several key aspects:

- **Flexible Time Perception**: Recognizing that time can expand or contract based on one's state of consciousness allows starseeds to navigate their daily routines more fluidly. This awareness can lead to a more relaxed approach to time, reducing stress and anxiety related to rigid schedules.

- **Synchronizing with Earth Time**: While starseeds may experience time differently, it's essential to synchronize with Earth's temporal rhythms for practical purposes, like meeting deadlines and maintaining relationships. Techniques such as grounding and setting intentions can help in this synchronization.

Applying Temporal Mechanics in Practical Scenarios

Temporal mechanics can be applied in various practical scenarios to enhance efficiency and well-being:

- **Time Management**: By tuning into their intuitive sense of time, starseeds can manage their tasks more effectively, often finding that they can accomplish more in less time when they're aligned with their higher selves.

- **Balancing Multiple Realities**: Starseeds might find themselves juggling responsibilities across different dimensions of reality. Learning to prioritize and compartmentalize these responsibilities can help maintain balance.

Temporal Mechanics and Wellness

Understanding and working with the malleable nature of time also have implications for personal wellness:

- **Mindfulness and Presence**: Practicing mindfulness and staying present can help starseeds navigate the temporal shifts they experience, reducing the disorientation and exhaustion that can come from rapid shifts in time perception.

- **Wellness Routines**: Incorporating wellness routines that honor both the physical and metaphysical aspects of existence can help starseeds maintain their health and energy levels. This might include meditation, yoga, and energy healing practices.

For hyperdimensional starseeds, mastering temporal mechanics is key to a harmonious existence. By integrating their multidimensional understanding of time with the practicalities of daily life, they can navigate their earthly journey with greater ease and purpose. This balance is not only essential for their personal well-being but also enables them to fulfill their mission on Earth more effectively. As we step into a new era of consciousness, the lessons learned from the temporal mechanics of starseeds can inspire us all to embrace a more fluid and intuitive approach to time.

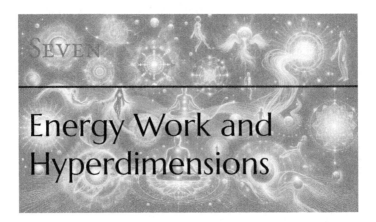

SEVEN
Energy Work and Hyperdimensions

Working with Kundalini Energy

Let's explore the profound concept of Kundalini energy, particularly its significance for hyperdimensional starseeds. Kundalini, often depicted as a coiled serpent lying dormant at the base of the spine, represents a potent source of spiritual and physical energy. When awakened, it can enhance one's multidimensional awareness and capabilities.

Understanding Kundalini in Hyperdimensional Context

Kundalini energy in hyperdimensional starseeds is often more active or accessible due to their intricate connection with multiple planes of existence. This energy, when harnessed properly, can aid in navigating these dimensions with greater ease and clarity.

- **Multidimensional Activation**: Kundalini serves as a bridge connecting the physical body to higher consciousness levels. Its activation can result in profound spiritual experiences and an expanded sense of awareness across different dimensions.

- **Physical and Spiritual Integration**: The awakening of Kundalini energy helps in the integration of physical and spiritual aspects, aligning the starseed's human experience with their cosmic purpose.

Awakening and Balancing Kundalini

The process of awakening Kundalini should be approached with respect and understanding due to its powerful nature.

- **Gradual Awakening**: It's crucial to awaken Kundalini gradually, under guidance, to avoid potential overwhelming experiences. Practices like yoga, meditation, and breathwork can facilitate this gradual and safe awakening.

- **Balancing Techniques**: Once awakened, maintaining balance is essential. Grounding techniques, chakra balancing, and regular spiritual practices can help in managing the potent energy flow.

Kundalini and Healing

Kundalini energy plays a vital role in the healing practices of hyperdimensional starseeds.

- **Self-Healing**: The rise of Kundalini can initiate profound healing, releasing blockages and traumas held in the physical and etheric bodies.

- **Healing Others**: Starseeds often use their awakened Kundalini energy in service of others, channeling it for healing and transformational purposes.

The awakening and management of Kundalini energy are pivotal for hyperdimensional starseeds. It enhances their connection to higher dimensions, aids in profound healing processes, and aligns their earthly existence with their multidimensional nature. We have emphasized the need for cautious and mindful engagement with Kundalini energy, ensuring a harmonious balance between the physical and spiritual realms. As starseeds continue to navigate their complex existence, Kundalini serves as a key to unlocking their full potential across all dimensions of reality.

Chakra Systems in Multiple Realities

Let's delve into the intricacies of the chakra systems as experienced by hyperdimensional starseeds. The chakras, known as energy centers within the body, play a pivotal role in the multidimensional experiences of these beings. Understanding and balancing these chakras is essential for starseeds to navigate multiple realities effectively.

Understanding the Chakra System in a Hyperdimensional Context

Chakras are not just limited to the physical body but extend into the etheric and astral bodies, impacting the starseed's experiences across various dimensions.

- **Multidimensional Chakra Activation**: Each chakra resonates with different dimensional energies. Starseeds often find that their chakras are more responsive or sensitive to these multidimensional frequencies.

- **The Extended Chakra System**: Beyond the traditional seven-chakra system, starseeds may experience additional chakras that connect them to higher dimensional energies, facilitating deeper cosmic integration.

Balancing and Aligning Chakras Across Dimensions

The process of aligning and balancing chakras is crucial for starseeds to maintain their multidimensional wellbeing.

- **Techniques for Alignment**: Practices like meditation, sound healing, and color therapy can be used to align and balance the chakras. These practices may vary in intensity and method, depending on the dimensional frequency the starseed is attuning to.

- **Challenges in Balancing**: Due to their sensitivity to multiple realities, starseeds might experience unique challenges in chakra alignment, such as overstimulation or blockages specific to certain dimensions.

Chakras and Their Roles in Multidimensional Journeys

Each chakra has a specific role in the starseed's journey across dimensions, influencing their physical, emotional, and spiritual experiences.

- **Root Chakra**: Grounding in multiple realities, ensuring stability and connection to the Earth plane.

- **Sacral Chakra**: Facilitating creative and sexual energies, enhancing experiences of joy and pleasure across dimensions.

- **Solar Plexus Chakra**: Empowering self-identity and willpower, critical in navigating dimensional shifts.

- **Heart Chakra**: The center for love and compassion, vital for interdimensional relationships and healing.

- **Throat Chakra**: Governing communication, crucial for expressing multidimensional truths.

- **Third Eye Chakra**: Enhancing intuition and psychic abilities, a key for perceiving beyond the physical realm.

- **Crown Chakra**: Connecting to higher consciousness and cosmic wisdom, essential for accessing higher dimensional knowledge.

For hyperdimensional starseeds, the chakra system is an essential framework for understanding and managing their energies across multiple dimensions. Proper care and balancing of the chakras enable these beings to maintain their physical, emotional, and spiritual health while exploring their vast multidimensional existence. By mastering the dynamics of their chakra systems, starseeds can effectively harness their energies to fulfill their missions across the cosmic spectrum, embodying their role as bridges between worlds.

Merkaba: Your Light Vehicle

Let's explore the concept of Merkaba, a term often associated with the spiritual and energetic fields of hyperdimensional starseeds. Merkaba, derived from ancient wisdom, symbolizes the chariot or light vehicle that facilitates interdimensional travel and spiritual ascension. Understanding Merkaba is crucial for starseeds navigating multiple realities, as it represents the synthesis of spirit and body powered by the energy of divine light.

Understanding Merkaba in Hyperdimensional Existence

Merkaba is more than just a concept; it is an energetic field that encompasses and transcends the physical and spiritual dimensions. In the context of hyperdimensional existence:

- **Energetic Geometry**: Merkaba is often visualized as two intersecting tetrahedrons, spinning in opposite directions, creating a three-dimensional energy field around the individual.

- **Connection with Higher Dimensions**: This energetic field serves as a conduit connecting starseeds with higher dimensions, allowing access to deeper wisdom and cosmic consciousness.

Activating and Utilizing the Merkaba

The activation of Merkaba is a profound spiritual practice that enables starseeds to navigate through different dimensions with greater awareness and purpose.

- **Meditative Practices**: Specific meditative techniques are employed to activate the Merkaba, often involving visualization, breathwork, and the recitation of sacred geometrical patterns.

- **Practical Applications**: Once activated, the Merkaba can be utilized for various purposes, including astral travel, healing, and accessing Akashic records. It serves as a protective field and aids in the alignment of physical, emotional, and spiritual bodies.

Merkaba and Its Role in Multidimensional Healing

Merkaba's significance extends beyond transportation across dimensions; it plays a crucial role in the healing processes of starseeds.

- **Energetic Alignment and Balance**: By activating the Merkaba, starseeds can achieve a profound level of energetic balance and alignment, essential for maintaining health across multiple dimensions.

- **Healing and Rejuvenation**: The Merkaba field can be used to channel higher-dimensional energies for healing, rejuvenation, and DNA activation, fostering holistic well-being.

Merkaba is a vital aspect of the hyperdimensional journey, serving as a vehicle for both spiritual ascension and interdimensional exploration. For starseeds, mastering the understanding and application of Merkaba is integral to their mission and evolution. It not only facilitates travel across dimensions but also offers a deeper connection with the cosmic consciousness and aids in the fulfillment of their soul's purpose across the multidimensional universe. The Merkaba, as a symbol of divine light and spiritual power, continues to be a beacon of guidance and transformation for those journeying through the complex tapestry of hyperdimensional existence.

Subtle Bodies and Auras

So let's now explore the intricate aspects of subtle bodies and auras, integral components of hyperdimensional existence for starseeds. These elements are not just mere energy fields but are reflective of the deeper spiritual, emotional, and mental states of a starseed. Understanding and harmonizing these layers are essential for navigating the complexities of multiple realities.

Understanding the Subtle Bodies

Subtle bodies are layers of energy that exist beyond the physical form, encompassing various dimensions of being. In hyperdimensional starseeds, these bodies are highly sensitive and responsive to multidimensional energies.

- **Ethereal Layers**: These include the etheric, emotional, mental, and spiritual layers, each corresponding to different aspects of existence and consciousness.

- **Interdimensional Interaction**: Subtle bodies interact with various dimensions, making them crucial for starseeds in understanding and adapting to different vibrational frequencies.

The Significance of Auras in Hyperdimensional Life

Auras are the energy fields that surround every living being, reflecting the condition of the subtle bodies. In starseeds, auras can provide deep insights into their multidimensional experiences.

- **Aura Colors and Meanings**: Different colors and hues in auras indicate various traits, emotions, and spiritual states. Understanding these colors can help starseeds decipher their own spiritual journey and challenges.

- **Auras as Diagnostic Tools**: Auras can be read and interpreted to diagnose imbalances or blockages in the subtle bodies, aiding in healing and energetic realignment.

Harmonizing and Healing Subtle Bodies and Auras

For starseeds, maintaining the health of their subtle bodies and auras is crucial for their multidimensional mission.

- **Energetic Practices**: Techniques like meditation, energy healing, and the use of crystals can help in cleansing and balancing the subtle bodies and auras.

- **Integration of Experiences**: Through regular attunement of their energy fields, starseeds can better integrate their experiences from different dimensions, leading to a more harmonious existence.

Subtle bodies and auras are more than just components of our energetic makeup; they are gateways to understanding our deeper selves and our connection to the cosmos. For hyperdimensional starseeds, mastering the knowledge and care of these aspects is not just beneficial but necessary for their journey across dimensions. By nurturing their subtle bodies and auras, starseeds can ensure that they are aligned, balanced, and prepared for the multifaceted experiences that their unique path entails. As they continue to evolve and ascend, their subtle bodies and auras serve as constant companions, reflecting their growth and transformation in the grand tapestry of multidimensional existence.

Soul Retrieval Across Dimensions

Let's do a deep dive into the profound process of soul retrieval, a practice essential for hyperdimensional starseeds who navigate multiple realities. Soul retrieval addresses the fragmentation of the soul that can occur through various experiences across dimensions. This healing journey is crucial for the integration and wholeness of the multidimensional self.

Understanding Soul Fragmentation

Soul fragmentation is a phenomenon where parts of the soul essence become disconnected or lost due to traumatic experiences, whether in the current lifetime or across multiple dimensions. For starseeds, this can happen more frequently due to their heightened sensitivity and expansive experiences across various realms.

- **Causes of Fragmentation**: Trauma, intense emotional experiences, or significant life changes can lead to fragmentation, especially when these events occur in alternate dimensions or past lives.

- **Symptoms and Indications**: Feelings of incompleteness, chronic emotional or physical ailments, and a persistent sense of searching for something unknown are common indicators of soul fragmentation.

The Process of Soul Retrieval

Soul retrieval is a healing practice aimed at locating, recovering, and reintegrating the lost parts of the soul.

- **Healing Techniques**: This process often involves deep meditative states, guided by practitioners skilled in navigating the multidimensional landscapes. Techniques can include shamanic journeys, past life regression, or intuitive energy work.

- **Reintegration and Healing**: Once fragments are retrieved, they are energetically reintegrated into the individual's aura. This integration is a delicate process that requires time, self-care, and often, the assistance of healing energies or entities.

Multidimensional Implications of Soul Retrieval

For starseeds, soul retrieval has implications beyond just the healing of the current self. It involves the reconciliation of experiences and traumas across various dimensions and lifetimes.

- **Restoring Multidimensional Wholeness**: Retrieving soul parts from different dimensions brings a sense of completeness and harmony to the starseed's multidimensional existence.

- **Enhancing Psychic Abilities and Connections**: As the soul becomes whole, starseeds often experience an enhancement in their psychic and intuitive abilities, deepening their connection to their higher selves and the cosmic consciousness.

Soul retrieval is a vital process for starseeds, addressing the unique challenges posed by their multifaceted existence across dimensions. By recognizing and healing the fragmentation of their soul, starseeds can achieve a more integrated, powerful, and harmonious state of being. This healing journey not only aids in their personal evolution but also enhances their ability to fulfill their cosmic missions, contributing to the greater balance and ascension of the universal consciousness. As they walk the path of soul retrieval, starseeds embody the true essence of their multidimensional selves, stepping into their power as beings of light and wisdom, woven intricately into the tapestry of the cosmos.

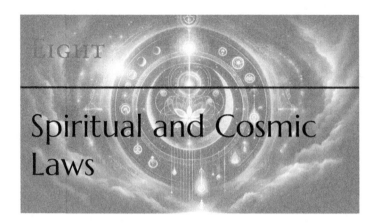

Spiritual and Cosmic Laws

The Karmic Influence

Let's explore the intricate concept of karma, especially as it pertains to starseeds navigating multiple realities. Karmic influence plays a pivotal role in the journey of a starseed, shaping their experiences and guiding their spiritual evolution across dimensions.

Understanding Karma in a Multidimensional Context

Karma, a term deeply rooted in Eastern philosophies, refers to the cause and effect principle where every action generates a force of energy that returns to us in kind. For starseeds, this principle extends beyond the physical realm, encompassing their actions and experiences across various dimensions and lifetimes.

- **Multidimensional Karma**: Unlike the traditional view of karma bound within a single lifetime, multidimensional karma includes the cumulative effects of actions and decisions made in different dimensions and existences.

- **Karmic Patterns**: Starseeds often carry karmic patterns that recur in various forms across dimensions, highlighting lessons that are yet to be learned or resolved.

Karmic Relationships and Soul Lessons

Starseeds frequently encounter karmic relationships and scenarios, which are essential for their growth and evolution.

- **Soul Contracts and Karmic Ties**: These are agreements made at the soul level, often before birth, involving other souls that play significant roles in one's multidimensional journey. Such contracts are meant to facilitate mutual growth and learning.

- **Learning Through Challenges**: Karmic lessons often manifest as challenges, pushing starseeds to confront and overcome recurring issues, thereby breaking cycles and evolving spiritually.

Transcending Karmic Cycles

The ultimate goal for starseeds in understanding and working with karma is to transcend these cycles, achieving a state of karmic resolution and balance.

- **Awareness and Acknowledgment**: Recognizing karmic patterns is the first step towards resolution. Awareness allows starseeds to consciously work through these cycles rather than being unconsciously driven by them.

- **Healing and Release**: Through various healing modalities such as meditation, energy work, and conscious decision-making, starseeds can release old karmic debts and patterns, facilitating a state of karmic liberation.

- **Progressing on the Spiritual Path**: As starseeds resolve their karmic cycles, they progress on their spiritual path, experiencing higher states of consciousness and deeper alignment with their cosmic missions.

The karmic influence in the lives of starseeds is a profound and pervasive force, extending across multiple dimensions and lifetimes. By understanding and working with these karmic patterns, starseeds can break free from recurring cycles, enabling them to evolve spiritually and fulfill their higher purposes. The journey through karma is not just about resolution but also about the realization of one's innate power to transcend limitations and embrace a more harmonious and enlightened existence. In mastering their karmic lessons, starseeds become beacons of light and wisdom, contributing to the collective evolution of consciousness across dimensions.

Law of One in Hyperdimensional Existence

Let's take a look at the Law of One, a central spiritual and cosmic law that significantly impacts the lives of hyperdimensional starseeds. The Law of One emphasizes the fundamental interconnectedness and unity of all existence across various dimensions, highlighting the idea that at the most profound level, all is one and one is all.

The Concept of Oneness in Multidimensional Realities

The Law of One transcends the concept of singularity as understood in the 3D perspective, expanding it into a multidimensional framework. This law suggests that every entity, every soul, and every particle of existence is intrinsically linked to each other, forming a vast, interconnected cosmic web.

- **Interconnectedness Across Dimensions**: This principle asserts that actions and events in one dimension resonate and have implications across others, due to the interconnected nature of all dimensions.

- **Unity Consciousness**: Starseeds often experience a profound sense of unity consciousness, a realization that individual consciousness is a part of a much larger, universal consciousness.

Implications for Starseeds

For starseeds, understanding and embodying the Law of One is essential in their journey across dimensions.

- **Harmonizing Multidimensional Existences**: Recognizing the interconnected nature of their various dimensional existences helps starseeds harmonize their experiences and lessons, leading to a more cohesive understanding of their multidimensional self.

- **Empathy and Compassion**: The awareness of oneness fosters a deeper sense of empathy and compassion towards other beings, as starseeds understand that helping others is essentially helping themselves.

The Law of One in Cosmic Evolution

The Law of One holds significant implications for the evolution of consciousness and the ascension process on a cosmic scale.

- **Collective Ascension**: The evolution of one affects the whole. Therefore, the spiritual growth and ascension of individual starseeds contribute to the collective ascension of all consciousness across dimensions.

- **Galactic and Universal Harmony**: As more beings align with the Law of One, it facilitates a harmonious existence across galaxies and dimensions, fostering peace, understanding, and unity on a cosmic level.

The Law of One is a fundamental principle that guides starseeds in their multidimensional journey, emphasizing the deep interconnection and unity of all existence. By understanding and embodying this law, starseeds not only advance in their own spiritual evolution but also contribute significantly to the collective evolution of consciousness across dimensions. The realization of oneness leads to a life filled with empathy, compassion, and a profound sense of connection with the cosmos, propelling starseeds and all beings towards a harmonious and enlightened existence. The Law of One serves as a reminder that in our essence, we are not just interconnected but are, in fact, one with the universe and each other.

The Principle of Correspondence

Let's delve into the Principle of Correspondence, a foundational concept within the realm of hyperdimensional existence. This principle, often encapsulated in the ancient Hermetic axiom "As above, so below; as below, so above", highlights the mirroring of macrocosmic and microcosmic realities. It underscores the interconnectedness between the various planes of existence and the individual's inner and outer worlds.

Understanding the Principle of Correspondence

The Principle of Correspondence posits that patterns, laws, and truths repeat throughout the cosmos, from the smallest atoms to the vastest galaxies. This universal law suggests that the microcosm reflects the macrocosm and vice versa.

- **Microcosm and Macrocosm**: The universe is a fractal structure where each part reflects the whole. The patterns we see in the greater universe are also evident within the smaller, individual realms.

- **Interdimensional Echoes**: This principle implies that events and experiences in one dimension or level of reality have a correspondence in another. This mirroring effect plays a significant role in the lives of starseeds who navigate multiple dimensions.

Applications in Hyperdimensional Life

The Principle of Correspondence is particularly relevant for starseeds, as they often experience a profound connection between their inner experiences and outer universal phenomena.

- **Personal Growth and Universal Evolution**: The spiritual development of a starseed is intimately connected to the evolution of the cosmos. Their personal transformation reflects and contributes to universal shifts.

- **Synchronicities**: Starseeds frequently encounter synchronicities, meaningful coincidences that are expressions of this principle. These synchronicities are signs of their alignment with the universal flow and a deeper interconnectedness with the cosmos.

Navigating Multiple Realities

For starseeds living in hyperdimensional realities, the Principle of Correspondence offers a framework to understand and navigate their complex experiences.

- **Harmony Across Dimensions**: By recognizing the correspondences between different dimensions, starseeds can harmonize their existence across these planes, leading to a more integrated and balanced life.

- **Guidance and Insight**: The principle can serve as a tool for gaining insights into the nature of reality and the interconnectedness of all things. It helps in understanding the underlying unity behind apparent diversities and complexities of the multiverse.

The Principle of Correspondence is a key concept in the journey of hyperdimensional starseeds, offering a profound understanding of the interconnectedness and reflection between the various levels of existence. By grasping this principle, starseeds can better comprehend their role in the cosmic tapestry and navigate their multidimensional lives with greater awareness and synchronicity. It serves as a reminder that the universe is a cohesive, interconnected whole, where each part, whether large or small, is a reflection of the other, weaving together the fabric of existence in a harmonious dance of cosmic correspondence.

Cosmic Justice and Dimensional Balance

We will now explore the intricate concept of Cosmic Justice and Dimensional Balance within the context of hyperdimensional existence and address how these principles play a vital role in the lives of starseeds and the functioning of the multiverse.

Understanding Cosmic Justice

Cosmic Justice refers to the universal and natural order that ensures balance and fairness across all dimensions and realities. Unlike human notions of justice, which are subjective and culturally defined, Cosmic Justice operates on a grander, more absolute scale.

- **Karmic Balance**: Central to Cosmic Justice is the idea of karma, the law of cause and effect. Actions, thoughts, and intentions ripple through dimensions, affecting the individual's journey across lifetimes and realities.

- **Divine Order**: Cosmic Justice is often perceived as a divine or natural order that maintains equilibrium in the cosmos. It's a system that transcends human law and operates independently of human morality or ethics.

Dimensional Balance

Dimensional Balance refers to the equilibrium between different dimensions and planes of existence. This balance is crucial for the stability of the universe and the evolution of consciousness.

- **Interdimensional Interplay**: Dimensional Balance involves a complex interplay between different realms. It ensures that energy, information, and consciousness flow harmoniously across dimensions.

- **Starseeds' Role**: Starseeds often play a key role in maintaining this balance. Their actions and decisions in one dimension can have profound effects on others, contributing to the overall harmony of the multiverse.

Navigating Cosmic Justice and Dimensional Balance

Starseeds, in their journey, must learn to navigate and understand these cosmic principles to live harmoniously across dimensions.

- **Ethical Considerations**: Understanding Cosmic Justice involves an ethical dimension, where starseeds must consider the impact of their actions not only in their current dimension but across the multiverse.

- **Alignment with Higher Purpose**: Aligning with one's higher purpose and the greater good of the cosmos is essential for maintaining Dimensional Balance. This alignment often requires a deep understanding of one's role in the cosmic plan.

The concepts of Cosmic Justice and Dimensional Balance offer starseeds a framework for understanding their place in the universe and the importance of their actions. These principles encourage a broader perspective that transcends individual desires and focuses on the greater cosmic order. By aligning with these cosmic laws, starseeds can contribute to the harmony and evolution of the multiverse, fostering a sense of unity and interconnectedness across all realms of existence. Understanding and integrating these principles are crucial steps in the journey of every starseed, paving the way for a more balanced and enlightened existence in the hyperdimensional tapestry of life.

Earth Missions: Grounding Multidimensional Light

So let's investigate delve into the profound topic of Earth Missions and the role of starseeds in grounding multidimensional ligh and examine the purpose and challenges faced by starseeds in their earthly incarnations and their contribution to the collective evolution of consciousness.

Understanding Earth Missions

Earth Missions refer to the specific roles or tasks that starseeds undertake during their incarnations on Earth. These missions are often aligned with their higher purpose and are crucial for both personal growth and the advancement of human consciousness.

- **Diversity of Missions**: Earth Missions vary widely among starseeds. Some may be called to be healers, teachers, or innovators, while others might work to anchor higher frequencies of energy into the Earth's matrix.

- **Alignment with Higher Self**: Successful completion of Earth Missions requires starseeds to stay aligned with their higher self, ensuring that their actions are in harmony with their soul's purpose.

Challenges in Earth Missions

Starseeds often encounter unique challenges while on their Earth Missions. These challenges are integral to their growth and the fulfillment of their objectives.

- **Navigating Density**: One of the primary challenges is navigating the dense energy of the Earth plane, which can be disorienting and overwhelming, especially for those accustomed to higher-dimensional existences.

- **Cultural and Societal Barriers**: Starseeds often face resistance from societal norms and cultural expectations, which can hinder their mission or lead to feelings of alienation.

Grounding Multidimensional Light

A critical aspect of many Earth Missions is to ground multidimensional light, which involves channeling higher frequencies of energy into the Earth's energetic grid.

- **Energetic Transmutation**: This process often requires transmuting lower vibrational energies into higher frequencies, facilitating the Earth's transition into a higher state of consciousness.

- **Collective Consciousness Evolution**: By grounding light, starseeds contribute to the awakening and evolution of the collective human consciousness, helping to shift paradigms and raise awareness on a global scale.

Earth Missions are a vital aspect of the hyperdimensional journey for starseeds. These missions are not only about the personal evolution of the starseeds but also about their contributions to the Earth and its inhabitants. By understanding their Earth Missions, starseeds can navigate their challenges more effectively and fulfill their role in grounding multidimensional light. Through these missions, starseeds play a pivotal role in the cosmic dance of evolution, ushering in a new era of awareness and enlightenment.

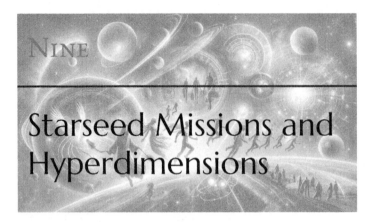

Nine

Starseed Missions and Hyperdimensions

The Purpose of Hyperdimensional Existence

So let's explore the profound and multifaceted topic of the purpose of hyperdimensional existence and delve into the deeper reasons behind the existence of starseeds in multiple dimensions and their significant role in the grand cosmic scheme.

Understanding the Purpose of Hyperdimensional Existence

Hyperdimensional existence is not a mere accident or a random occurrence in the vast expanse of the universe. It serves a greater purpose that intertwines with the evolution of consciousness and the expansion of the universe.

- **Evolution of Consciousness**: One of the primary purposes of hyperdimensional existence is the evolution and elevation of consciousness across different dimensions. Starseeds, as part of this existence, play a crucial role in infusing higher dimensional consciousness into lower dimensions, like Earth.

- **Cosmic Harmony and Balance**: Hyperdimensional beings contribute to maintaining cosmic harmony and balance. Their presence across dimensions ensures the flow and exchange of energy and information, crucial for the stability of the multiverse.

The Role of Starseeds in Hyperdimensional Existence

Starseeds are not just passive observers but active participants in the cosmic play. Their roles are diverse and critical to the unfolding of the universal narrative.

- **Bridging Dimensions**: Starseeds act as bridges between different dimensions, bringing forth knowledge, wisdom, and energy from higher realms to the physical world.

- **Catalysts for Change**: Often, starseeds are catalysts for significant changes, initiating or accelerating evolutionary shifts on the planets and dimensions they inhabit.

The Greater Cosmic Plan

The hyperdimensional existence of starseeds is intricately linked to a greater cosmic plan, a design that is beyond the comprehension of singular dimensional consciousness.

- **Interconnectedness with All Life**: Starseeds, through their multidimensional nature, are deeply interconnected with all forms of life across the universe. This interconnectedness is key to understanding the holistic nature of their mission.

- **Contribution to Universal Expansion**: The experiences, lessons, and growth attained by starseeds in various dimensions contribute to the overall expansion and enrichment of the universe. Their journey is not just personal but also universal.

The purpose of hyperdimensional existence transcends individual experiences and ventures into the realm of universal significance. For starseeds, understanding this purpose is vital to fulfilling their missions and contributing effectively to the cosmic narrative. We have offered a broader perspective on why starseeds exist across multiple dimensions and how their presence is integral to the grand design of the cosmos. By comprehending their role in this larger context, starseeds can navigate their journeys with greater clarity, purpose, and dedication to the collective evolution of all existence.

Earth Missions: Grounding Multidimensional Light

Let's delve into the significant role of hyperdimensional starseeds in their Earth missions, focusing on how they ground multidimensional light into our planet. This process is essential in the collective evolution of Earth's consciousness and aids in the transformative journey of humanity.

The Nature of Earth Missions

Earth missions undertaken by starseeds are multifaceted and deeply intertwined with the spiritual evolution of the planet. These missions involve channeling and anchoring higher-dimensional energies into the Earth's energetic grid.

- **Channeling Higher Energies**: Starseeds serve as conduits for higher frequencies, bringing in advanced knowledge, wisdom, and vibrational upliftment.

- **Anchoring the Light**: They play a critical role in grounding this higher vibrational energy, integrating it with the Earth's energy field to facilitate global consciousness shifts.

The Impact of Grounding Multidimensional Light

The process of grounding multidimensional light has profound effects on the planet, contributing to both energetic and physical changes.

- **Raising Planetary Vibration**: By anchoring higher frequencies, starseeds help in elevating the overall vibrational state of the planet, making it more conducive to spiritual awakening and growth.

- **Catalyzing Evolutionary Shifts**: This higher vibration facilitates significant evolutionary leaps, both in human consciousness and in the physical environment.

Challenges and Responsibilities

Starseeds on Earth missions often face unique challenges and carry immense responsibilities, pivotal to the success of their tasks.

- **Navigating Density**: One of the significant challenges is the dense vibrational environment of Earth, which can create a sense of disconnection from their higher-dimensional origins.

- **Maintaining Integrity**: Starseeds must maintain their vibrational integrity, often requiring them to be resilient in the face of Earth's collective consciousness's denser aspects.

Starseeds' Earth missions are integral to the planet's ongoing shift into higher consciousness realms. By grounding multidimensional light, these beings contribute significantly to the spiritual evolution of Earth and its inhabitants. Their role, while fraught with challenges, is a testament to their resilience and dedication to the cosmic plan of awakening and transformation.

Galactic Diplomacy Across Dimensions

Let's investigate the pivotal role of hyperdimensional starseeds in Galactic Diplomacy, a crucial aspect of their mission that involves navigating and fostering relationships across various dimensions and galactic communities.

The Essence of Galactic Diplomacy

Galactic Diplomacy refers to the complex interactions and negotiations between different dimensional entities, star systems, and galactic civilizations. It aims to maintain harmony, share knowledge, and collaborate for the greater good of all involved parties.

- **Interstellar Communication**: Starseeds often act as intermediaries, facilitating communication between Earth and other galactic civilizations.

- **Peacekeeping and Mediation**: They play a role in resolving conflicts and misunderstandings that may arise between different dimensional entities.

Roles and Responsibilities

The involvement in Galactic Diplomacy requires starseeds to possess certain qualities and fulfill specific roles:

- **Ambassadors of Earth**: Representing Earth in the galactic community, starseeds convey human perspectives and aspirations, helping to integrate Earth more fully into the galactic family.

- **Harbingers of Universal Harmony**: They strive to promote unity and understanding, transcending differences and fostering a sense of oneness among diverse cosmic cultures.

Challenges in Galactic Diplomacy

Engaging in diplomacy across dimensions is not without its challenges, which starseeds must adeptly navigate:

- **Navigating Cultural Differences**: Understanding

and respecting the vastly different cultures, beliefs, and customs of various galactic civilizations can be daunting.

- **Dealing with Complex Agendas**: Starseeds must be discerning and wise in dealing with the various agendas of different cosmic entities, ensuring that the higher good is always the priority.

Galactic Diplomacy is a critical component of the starseeds' mission, requiring a deep understanding of cosmic law, interstellar cultures, and the delicate balance of power within the multiverse. Through their efforts, starseeds help to weave a tapestry of peace and cooperation, not just on Earth but across the cosmos.

Facilitators of Dimensional Transitions

Let's delve into the role of hyperdimensional starseeds as facilitators of dimensional transitions. These transitions are pivotal moments when individuals, societies, or even entire planets shift from one level of consciousness and existence to another, more advanced state. Starseeds, with their deep understanding of multidimensional realities, play a critical role in guiding these transitions.

Understanding Dimensional Transitions

Dimensional transitions involve a profound change in consciousness and reality perception. They can occur on a personal level, within communities, or on a planetary scale. These transitions are not just physical shifts but involve spiritual, mental, and emotional transformation.

- **Significance of Transitions**: These are evolutionary leaps that bring about significant changes in understanding and interacting with the universe.

- **Manifestations of Transitions**: They can manifest as shifts in societal values, technological advancements, or enhanced spiritual awareness.

Role of Starseeds in Transitions

Starseeds, due to their inherent connection with multiple dimensions, play a crucial role in facilitating these transitions:

- **Guides and Teachers**: They provide guidance and knowledge to those undergoing transitions, helping them navigate the challenges and opportunities these changes bring.

- **Catalysts for Change**: Their presence and actions often serve as catalysts for transitions, accelerating the evolution of consciousness in their surroundings.

Challenges in Facilitating Transitions

Facilitating dimensional transitions is not without challenges:

- **Resistance to Change**: Starseeds often encounter resistance from individuals or systems unwilling to embrace change or let go of outdated paradigms.

- **Balancing Different Realities**: Managing the complexities of existing in multiple realities while guiding others through transitions requires exceptional wisdom and balance.

The role of starseeds as facilitators of dimensional transitions is vital in the evolutionary journey of consciousness. Their ability to navigate and bridge various realms of existence enables them to guide others through these transformative processes and this highlights their invaluable contribution to the cosmic evolution, marking them as essential agents of change in the grand scheme of multidimensional existence. Their work ensures that transitions are not only successful but also harmonious, leading to a more interconnected and enlightened universe.

Healing Missions in Parallel Realities

Let's take a deep dive into the profound work of hyperdimensional starseeds involved in healing missions across parallel realities. These missions are not only about physical healing but also encompass emotional, spiritual, and cosmic healing, addressing the multi-layered aspects of existence across various dimensions.

The Nature of Healing Across Dimensions

Healing in hyperdimensional terms transcends the conventional understanding of the word. It involves a harmonization of energies across multiple levels of existence.

- **Multidimensional Healing**: This form of healing

recognizes the interconnectedness of physical, emotional, spiritual, and energetic planes.

- **Restoring Balance**: The primary goal is to restore balance and harmony in all realms of existence, acknowledging the ripple effect across dimensions.

Starseeds as Healers

Starseeds, with their innate connection to multiple dimensions, are naturally attuned to the healing frequencies needed in different realms.

- **Empathic Abilities**: Many starseeds possess heightened empathic abilities, allowing them to sense disharmony and imbalance across dimensions.

- **Healing Techniques**: They employ a variety of healing techniques, from energy work and vibrational healing to advanced spiritual practices that transcend conventional methods.

Healing Missions: Challenges and Triumphs

Healing missions are often fraught with challenges, as starseeds navigate complex energetic landscapes and confront deep-seated imbalances.

- **Navigating Resistance**: Encountering resistance, both from entities within the dimensions being healed and from external forces, is a common challenge.

- **Transformative Impact**: Despite the hurdles, the healing work of starseeds has a transformative impact, often leading to profound shifts in consciousness and vibrational upliftment.

The healing missions undertaken by hyperdimensional starseeds in parallel realities are vital for the overall health and evolution of the cosmos. These missions, while challenging, contribute significantly to the restoration of balance and harmony across dimensions. By addressing issues at a multidimensional level, starseeds play a crucial role in facilitating the healing and ascension of not just individuals but entire realms of existence. Their work is a testament to the interconnected nature of all life and the power of healing as a force for cosmic evolution.

Galactic Heritage and Lineages

Arcturian Multidimensional Technologies

The Arcturian Legacy

In the vast expanse of the cosmos, the Arcturian star system holds a unique position in the context of hyperdimensional realities. Known for their advanced technologies and profound spiritual wisdom, Arcturians are considered as one of the most evolved civilizations in our galaxy. Their contribution to hyperdimensional understanding is primarily through their sophisticated technologies, which are not just mechanical but also deeply spiritual and consciousness-expanding.

Arcturian technologies are believed to operate at the convergence of science and spirituality, transcending the limitations of traditional physical laws. These technologies are based on the principles of quantum mechanics, sacred geometry, and the harnessing of cosmic energies. They are designed to facilitate deep healing, consciousness expansion, and the exploration of different dimensions.

Arcturian Multidimensional Technologies

Arcturian technologies are multifaceted, each serving a unique purpose in aiding starseeds and other beings in their evolutionary journey:

Healing Chambers: These are believed to be spaces where advanced healing processes occur. Utilizing a combination of energy frequencies, light, and advanced spiritual techniques, these chambers are said to work at cellular and soul levels, facilitating profound healing and rejuvenation.

Light Ships: Often mentioned in starseed narratives, Arcturian light ships are not just modes of transportation but also serve as floating sanctuaries of higher learning and healing. These ships are said to travel through various dimensions and are equipped with advanced healing technologies.

Crystalline Grids: Arcturians are known for their expertise in creating and maintaining crystalline grids. These grids are energetic constructs that help in the stabilization of Earth's energy fields and also act as transmitters of high-frequency cosmic energies.

Integration with Human Consciousness

The interaction of Arcturian technologies with human consciousness is a key aspect of their role in the hyperdimensional tapestry. These technologies are not just external tools but are designed to interact intimately with the consciousness of the user. This interaction is said to trigger awakenings, unlock psychic abilities, and even facilitate interdimensional travel.

Consciousness Expansion: Arcturian technologies are believed to assist in the expansion of consciousness, helping beings to access higher states of awareness and deeper understanding of the cosmic laws.

DNA Activation: It's proposed that these technologies can interact with the human DNA, activating dormant parts which are linked to higher dimensional awareness and abilities.

Enhancing Psychic Abilities: Regular interaction with these technologies is said to enhance psychic abilities like telepathy, clairvoyance, and astral projection, enabling a more profound connection with the higher dimensions.

In essence, Arcturian multidimensional technologies represent a convergence of spiritual wisdom and advanced science. Their role in the hyperdimensional journey of starseeds and other beings is pivotal, providing tools and experiences that facilitate deeper understanding, healing, and evolution. The Arcturian legacy, thus, is not just about their technological advancements, but about the holistic integration of these technologies with the spiritual growth and multidimensional evolution of consciousness.

Pleiades and Emotional Mastery

The Pleiadian Connection

The Pleiadian star cluster, also known as the Seven Sisters, is a prominent feature in the night sky and has a special significance in the hyperdimensional context. The beings from the Pleiades, commonly referred to as Pleiadians, are thought to possess a deep understanding of emotional and spiritual realms. Their connection with Earth and humanity is often centered around themes of healing, growth, and emotional mastery. Pleiadians are believed to be nurturing and compassionate, offering wisdom that helps in the evolution of consciousness and the harmonization of emotions.

Emotional Mastery in Hyperdimensional Realities

Emotional mastery, as taught by the Pleiadians, is not just about managing emotions in a conventional sense. It is about understanding the intricate relationship between emotions and multidimensional existence. Emotions are seen as powerful energies that can influence our reality, shape our experiences across dimensions, and impact our spiritual journey.

Navigating Emotional Landscapes: Pleiadian teachings emphasize the importance of becoming aware of and navigating through one's emotional landscape. This involves recognizing emotions as indicators of vibrational states and using them as tools for spiritual growth and dimensional alignment.

Healing Emotional Trauma: Pleiadians are known for their healing abilities, particularly in the realm of emotional and soul-level trauma. They advocate for deep inner work to release and heal past wounds, which is essential for advancing in hyperdimensional awareness.

Elevating Emotional Frequencies: Pleiadians teach methods to elevate emotional frequencies, transforming lower vibrational emotions like fear and anger into higher states such as love and joy. This elevation is key to accessing higher dimensions and maintaining a harmonious existence within them.

Pleiadian Practices for Emotional Mastery

To facilitate emotional mastery, Pleiadians offer various practices and insights. These practices are designed to align individuals with higher dimensional frequencies and bring about profound inner transformations.

Meditation and Mindfulness: Pleiadians emphasize the practice of meditation and mindfulness as tools for emotional regulation and awareness. These practices help in attuning to higher frequencies and cultivating a state of inner peace and clarity.

Heart-Centered Living: A core Pleiadian teaching is living from the heart space. This involves making decisions and reacting to situations from a place of love and compassion, rather than fear or ego.

Connection with Nature: Pleiadians advocate for a strong connection with nature as a means to balance and harmonize emotions. Nature is seen as a reflection of the cosmic order and a source of profound healing energy.

The Pleiadian perspective on emotional mastery in hyperdimensional realities offers a path to spiritual evolution through the understanding and transformation of emotions. By learning to navigate, heal, and elevate our emotional states, we align more closely with higher dimensions, paving the way for a more harmonious and enlightened existence. The Pleiadian teachings, with their emphasis on heart-centered living, meditation, and a deep connection with nature, provide valuable guidance for those seeking to explore the multidimensional aspects of their being.

Lyran Wisdom and Starseed Lineages

The Legacy of Lyra

In the tapestry of cosmic lineages, Lyra holds a unique and ancient position, often considered as the cradle of humanoid consciousness in the galaxy. The star system of Lyra, with its rich history and spiritual depth, offers profound insights into the journey of starseeds and the evolution of consciousness across dimensions. Lyrans, the beings from this star system, are characterized by their deep wisdom, strong connection to higher spiritual realms, and advanced understanding of cosmic principles.

Lyran Teachings on Multidimensional Existence

Lyrans offer a perspective on existence that is deeply intertwined with the concepts of spirituality and cosmic unity. Their teachings are centered around understanding the multidimensional nature of reality and our place within it.

Cosmic Awareness: Lyran teachings emphasize the importance of cosmic awareness - understanding one's existence beyond the physical realm. They encourage exploring the soul's journey across various dimensions and incarnations.

Harmony with Universal Laws: Lyrans are believed to be masters of understanding and aligning with the Universal Laws, such as the Law of One and the Law of Correspondence. They advocate for living in a way that is in harmony with these cosmic principles.

Vibrational Resonance: A key aspect of Lyran wisdom is the understanding of vibrational resonance and its role in shaping reality. They teach that by aligning one's personal vibration with higher frequencies, one can access greater wisdom and multidimensional experiences.

The Role of Lyran Starseeds

Lyran starseeds, those who originate from or are connected to the Lyran star system, have specific roles and characteristics in their earthly incarnation:

Wisdom Keepers: Many Lyran starseeds are seen as wisdom keepers, carrying deep spiritual knowledge and cosmic insights. They often find themselves in roles of teaching and guiding others on their spiritual paths.

Healers of the Heart and Soul: With their profound understanding of emotional and spiritual realms, Lyran starseeds are natural healers. They possess the ability to facilitate deep emotional healing and spiritual growth in others.

Architects of Society: Lyrans are often involved in laying down the foundational structures of societies, be it through innovative ideas, spiritual teachings, or leading by example. They bring forth concepts of unity, equality, and higher consciousness.

Integrating Lyran Wisdom in Daily Life

For those drawn to the Lyran lineage, integrating their wisdom into daily life involves a few key practices:

Meditation and Contemplation: Regular meditation helps in attuning to the Lyran energies and accessing the wisdom they offer. Contemplation on cosmic truths aids in internalizing these teachings.

Living Authentically: Lyrans advocate for living a life that is true to one's soul's purpose, free from societal conditioning and in alignment with higher spiritual principles.

Promoting Unity and Harmony: Embodying the Lyran teachings involves working towards greater unity and harmony, both within oneself and in the external world.

The Lyran star system, with its ancient wisdom and spiritual depth, offers invaluable insights for starseeds navigating the complexities of multidimensional existence. The teachings of the Lyrans encourage a deep exploration of the soul's journey, alignment with cosmic laws, and living a life resonant with higher vibrations. Lyran starseeds, as wisdom keepers and healers, play a significant role in the spiritual evolution of humanity, guiding us towards a more unified and conscious existence.

Andromedan Perspective on Hyperdimensions

The Essence of Andromedan Teachings

The Andromeda Galaxy, a spiral galaxy approximately 2.5 million light-years from Earth, is believed to be home to advanced civilizations with profound spiritual and multidimensional knowledge. Andromedan beings, known for their evolved technological and spiritual advancements, offer unique perspectives on living and navigating through multiple dimensions. Their teachings emphasize the interconnectedness of all existence, the importance of balance and harmony, and the evolution towards higher consciousness.

Understanding Multidimensionality Through Andromedan Eyes

Andromedan philosophy provides a broad understanding of the nature of reality, where multiple dimensions coexist and interact in a complex, yet harmonious, cosmic dance.

Interdimensional Connectivity: Andromedans perceive reality as a web of interconnected dimensions, each existing simultaneously and influencing each other. They teach that actions in one dimension can have ripples across others, emphasizing the importance of conscious living.

The Evolution of Consciousness: Central to Andromedan thought is the evolution of consciousness through different dimensions. They believe that each dimension offers unique lessons and opportunities for growth, contributing to the soul's overall development.

Harmony and Balance: Andromedans stress the importance of maintaining harmony and balance, not just within individual dimensions, but across them. They view this balance as crucial for the health of the cosmos and the evolution of all beings within it.

The Role of Andromedan Starseeds in Human Evolution

Starseeds who resonate with the Andromedan frequency often find themselves drawn to roles that involve bringing harmony and higher wisdom to Earth. They are typically characterized by their deep empathy, visionary outlook, and a strong sense of cosmic unity.

Bringers of Harmony: Andromedan starseeds often have a natural ability to mediate conflicts and bring about resolution. Their presence can have a calming and unifying effect in tumultuous situations.

Visionaries and Innovators: With their advanced understanding of technology and spirituality, Andromedan starseeds are often at the forefront of innovative thinking, blending science and spirituality in unique ways.

Guides to Higher Consciousness: These starseeds serve as guides and mentors, helping others to raise their consciousness and understand the deeper truths of the universe.

Integrating Andromedan Wisdom into Daily Life

Embracing Andromedan teachings involves incorporating their principles into everyday life, leading to a more conscious and harmonious existence.

Living Consciously: Andromedans encourage living with awareness of the impact of one's actions across dimensions. This involves making choices that are in alignment with higher principles of love, unity, and balance.

Embracing Unity in Diversity: Recognizing the interconnectedness of all beings, regardless of their dimensional origin, is a key aspect of Andromedan philosophy. They advocate for unity amidst diversity, seeing the strength in different perspectives and experiences.

Harmonizing Technology and Spirituality: Andromedans teach the harmonious integration of technology and spirituality. This involves using technology in ways that uplift and evolve consciousness rather than exploiting or harming.

The Andromedan perspective on hyperdimensions offers insightful guidance on understanding the complex nature of reality and our role within it. Their teachings highlight the importance of interdimensional connectivity, the evolution of consciousness, and the need for harmony and balance. Andromedan starseeds, with their unique attributes and roles, contribute significantly to the collective evolution of humanity, guiding us towards a future where technology and spirituality are harmoniously integrated for the greater good of the cosmos.

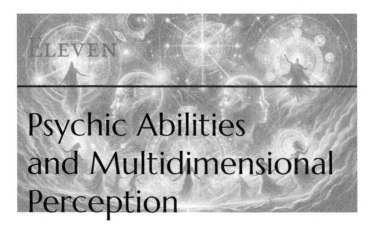

Psychic Abilities and Multidimensional Perception

Telepathy and Interspecies Communication

The Realm of Telepathic Exchange

Telepathy, a form of communication that transcends verbal and written languages, is deeply embedded in the realm of hyperdimensional realities. This non-verbal, mind-to-mind exchange of thoughts, ideas, and feelings is not just confined to interactions among humans but extends to interspecies communication as well. In a hyperdimensional context, telepathy is more than a psychic phenomenon; it's a fundamental means of connecting and understanding beings across different dimensions and states of consciousness.

Understanding and Developing Telepathic Abilities

Telepathy is not exclusive to a select few; rather, it's a latent ability present in all beings, awaiting activation and cultivation.

Awakening Telepathic Abilities: The journey to developing telepathic abilities begins with the recognition of the interconnected nature of all consciousness. Practices like meditation, mindfulness, and focused intention-setting can awaken and enhance telepathic skills.

Cultivating Clarity and Empathy: Effective telepathic communication requires a clear mind and a compassionate heart. Cultivating these qualities enables a deeper and more accurate transmission of thoughts and emotions.

Practice and Patience: Like any skill, telepathy requires consistent practice. This involves exercises in sending and receiving thoughts, starting with simple ideas and gradually moving to more complex concepts.

Interspecies Communication: Beyond Human Boundaries

Interspecies communication, an extension of telepathy, involves connecting with the consciousness of other species, understanding their perspectives, and exchanging information with them. This form of communication is pivotal in hyperdimensional realities, where the understanding and harmony between different forms of life are essential.

Connecting with Animal Consciousness: This involves tuning into the frequency of animals, understanding their emotional and mental states, and communicating with them in a respectful and non-intrusive manner.

Plant and Elemental Communication: Beyond animals, telepathy extends to communicating with plants and elemental beings. This form of communication often reveals profound insights about the natural world and its intricate ecosystems.

Galactic and Interdimensional Beings: Advanced practitioners of telepathy may also establish communication with beings from other dimensions or star systems, gaining cosmic wisdom and insights into universal truths.

The Role of Telepathy in Hyperdimensional Existence

In a hyperdimensional context, telepathy plays several crucial roles:

Fostering Understanding and Unity: Telepathy bridges the gap between different species and dimensions, fostering a deeper understanding and a sense of unity among all forms of life.

Navigating Multidimensional Realities: Telepathic abilities are essential tools for navigating and interacting within multidimensional realities. They enable an exchange of knowledge and guidance essential for multidimensional travel and exploration.

Enhancing Spiritual Growth: Telepathic communication is not just about exchanging information; it's a spiritual practice that enhances one's consciousness and contributes to overall spiritual growth.

Telepathy and interspecies communication are integral aspects of hyperdimensional existence. They represent the potential of consciousness to transcend physical and dimensional boundaries, enabling a profound and harmonious exchange between diverse forms of life. The development and practice of these abilities pave the way for a more interconnected and empathetic existence, both on Earth and in the broader cosmic context.

Clairvoyance in a Multidimensional Context

The Facets of Clairvoyance

Clairvoyance, often described as 'clear seeing,' is a psychic ability that allows one to perceive and gain information beyond the limitations of the physical senses. In the realm of hyperdimensional existence, clairvoyance takes on a multidimensional aspect, enabling individuals to see across different dimensions and timeframes. This form of perception is not just about foreseeing the future but encompasses a broad spectrum of visionary experiences, including seeing auras, energy patterns, and even entities from other dimensions.

Developing Multidimensional Clairvoyance

The journey to developing clairvoyant abilities, particularly in a multidimensional context, involves a combination of innate talent, dedicated practice, and the right guidance.

Meditative Practices: Regular meditation is crucial in opening up the third eye chakra, the energy center associated with clairvoyance. Techniques that focus on visualizing and energizing the third eye can gradually awaken clairvoyant abilities.

Cultivation of Inner Sight: Developing clairvoyance requires honing one's inner vision. This involves trusting and interpreting the mental images and visions that come during meditation or in a relaxed state of mind.

Psychic Training and Guidance: Learning from experienced mentors or undergoing psychic development training can accelerate the process of developing clairvoyant abilities. These teachings often provide structured exercises and insights into interpreting visions correctly.

Clairvoyance in Hyperdimensional Work

In the context of hyperdimensional realities, clairvoyance plays several vital roles:

Navigating Between Dimensions: Clairvoyants can perceive the vibrational frequencies of different dimensions, aiding in interdimensional travel and exploration.

Energy Diagnosis and Healing: Many clairvoyants use their abilities to diagnose energetic imbalances or blockages, both in physical bodies and in the subtle energy fields. This skill is particularly valuable in energy healing practices.

Understanding Cosmic Patterns: Clairvoyance enables one to see and understand the larger cosmic patterns at play, providing insights into the interconnectedness of all things and the underlying unity of the cosmos.

Challenges and Ethical Considerations

While clairvoyance is a powerful tool, it comes with its own set of challenges and ethical considerations:

Interpretation and Accuracy: One of the major challenges in clairvoyance is correctly interpreting the visions and symbols received. Misinterpretation can lead to confusion or misguidance.

Psychic Overload: Without proper grounding and protection, clairvoyants may experience psychic overload, where they are overwhelmed by the influx of visual information.

Ethical Responsibility: Clairvoyants must adhere to a strong ethical code, especially regarding privacy and consent when viewing into others' lives or energy fields.

Clairvoyance in a multidimensional context is a profound and expansive ability that offers deeper insights into the nature of reality and the unseen world. Its development requires a mix of meditative practices, psychic training, and ethical mindfulness. As clairvoyants navigate through the layers of multidimensional existence, they play a crucial role in the understanding and healing processes, contributing significantly to the collective evolution of consciousness.

Precognition and Future Realities

Understanding Precognition in a Hyperdimensional Context

Precognition, the ability to perceive or predict future events, is a profound aspect of psychic awareness, especially within the framework of hyperdimensional realities. In this broader context, precognition is not merely foresight but a complex interaction with the fluid nature of time and the multitude of potential futures that exist in the quantum field. This capability extends beyond linear time, allowing one to access, perceive, and sometimes influence possible future outcomes.

The Mechanics of Precognitive Perception

Precognition operates on the principle that time is not a fixed linear progression but a dynamic, multi-layered continuum. This understanding opens up several key aspects:

Quantum Potentialities: Precognition taps into the realm of quantum possibilities, where multiple potential futures exist simultaneously. This access is not deterministic but offers glimpses into the probable paths that events might take.

Intuitive Connection: The ability to perceive future events often manifests through intuitive senses. It can come as spontaneous insights, dreams, visions, or a deep inner knowing.

Synchronicity and Alignment: Precognitive experiences are often linked to a state of synchronicity with the universe, where one is deeply aligned with the flow of cosmic energies and the interconnected web of existence.

Developing and Honing Precognitive Skills

Enhancing precognitive abilities involves several practices and attitudes:

Meditative and Mindfulness Practices: Regular meditation helps in attuning to the higher frequencies where precognitive insights are more readily accessible. Mindfulness in daily life fosters a receptive state of mind.

Trust and Interpretation: Developing trust in one's intuitive insights is crucial. Equally important is learning to interpret these insights correctly, distinguishing between true precognitive messages and normal mental chatter.

Ethical Awareness: With the power to perceive potential futures comes the responsibility to use this knowledge ethically, respecting free will and the natural course of events.

The Role of Precognition in Hyperdimensional Life

In the context of hyperdimensional existence, precognition serves several key roles:

Navigating Timelines: Precognitive insights can assist starseeds and others in navigating through the complex web of timelines, helping to make choices that align with desired outcomes.

Spiritual Growth and Understanding: Engaging with potential futures can lead to profound spiritual insights, understanding the nature of reality, and the role of consciousness in shaping it.

Collective Evolution: Precognitive abilities can contribute to the collective evolution of consciousness by foreseeing and guiding towards pathways that lead to beneficial outcomes for humanity and the planet.

Challenges and Ethical Considerations

While precognition is a powerful tool, it comes with its own set of challenges:

Emotional and Psychological Impact: Regular precognitive experiences can be emotionally taxing, especially when they pertain to negative or challenging events.

Accuracy and Misinterpretation: Not all precognitive visions will come to pass as perceived. The fluid nature of time means that futures can change based on current actions and decisions.

Ethical Responsibility: It's crucial to use precognitive insights with discretion, especially when they involve other people's lives and choices.

Precognition within hyperdimensional realities offers a unique window into the potentials of future events and pathways. By developing and responsibly using precognitive abilities, individuals can gain profound insights into the nature of time, make informed decisions that align with desired outcomes, and contribute positively to the collective evolution of consciousness. The journey of honing these skills is as much about personal growth as it is about understanding the deeper cosmic interplay of time and reality.

Psychometry and Dimensional Residue

The Essence of Psychometry

Psychometry, known as the psychic ability to read information from objects, is a fascinating aspect of multidimensional perception. This skill involves touching or being in proximity to an object and receiving intuitive impressions about its history, previous owners, and events associated with it. In the context of hyperdimensional realities, psychometry extends beyond simple object reading; it becomes a gateway to understanding the layered histories and energies embedded in physical matter across various dimensions.

Understanding Dimensional Residue

Dimensional residue refers to the energetic imprints left on objects or locations due to significant events or emotional experiences. These residues can linger across time and dimensions, creating a tapestry of historical and energetic information.

Energetic Imprints: Objects and places absorb the energies of their surroundings. Significant events, especially those charged with strong emotions, leave potent imprints that can be perceived psychometrically.

Temporal Echoes: Psychometry in a hyperdimensional context involves not just reading the past but also sensing the echoes of potential futures, as objects resonate with the energies of possible timelines.

Dimensional Overlaps: Objects that have existed in multiple dimensions may carry imprints from these experiences, offering insights into parallel realities and alternate existences.

Developing Psychometric Abilities

Developing psychometric skills involves a combination of natural psychic ability, training, and practice.

Sensory Attunement: The first step is to attune one's senses to subtle energies. This can be achieved through meditation, mindfulness, and energy work practices.

Practice and Interpretation: Regular practice with different objects and environments enhances the ability to discern and interpret the myriad impressions received.

Ethical Considerations: Respect for privacy and ethical use of psychometry is paramount. It's important to seek permission when reading objects that belong to others.

Applications in Hyperdimensional Work

Psychometry can be applied in various contexts within hyperdimensional work:

Historical Insight and Research: Psychometry can reveal hidden histories and forgotten stories, contributing to archaeological and historical research, especially in understanding ancient civilizations and their multidimensional connections.

Healing and Energy Work: Understanding the energetic history of an object or place can be crucial in healing work, helping to clear negative residues or harmonize energies.

Exploring Past Lives and Timelines: Objects with historical significance can act as portals to past life experiences or alternate timelines, offering profound insights into one's soul journey and the interconnectedness of time and space.

Challenges and Growth

Psychometric exploration comes with its own challenges:

Emotional Overwhelm: Encountering intense or traumatic energies can be emotionally overwhelming. Developing grounding and shielding techniques is essential.

Accuracy and Interpretation: Differentiating between one's own thoughts and actual psychometric impressions requires practice and discernment.

Ethical Boundaries: Maintaining ethical boundaries and respecting the sanctity of individual and collective histories is crucial.

Psychometry, especially within the scope of hyperdimensional realities, offers a unique lens to perceive and interact with the multi-layered tapestry of existence. It bridges the gap between the physical and the metaphysical, between past, present, and potential futures. By honing psychometric skills, one can gain deeper insights into the fabric of reality, contributing to a more profound understanding of the universe and our place within it.

Dimensional Dreamwork

The Power of Dreams in Multidimensional Exploration

Dreams have always been a source of mystery and fascination, but in the context of hyperdimensional realities, they take on a new significance. Dimensional dreamwork refers to the practice of using dreams as portals to access and explore different dimensions of existence. This practice goes beyond traditional dream interpretation, delving into the realms of astral travel, soul journeying, and interdimensional communication.

Understanding the Multidimensional Nature of Dreams

Dreams are not just random firings of the sleeping brain; they are complex experiences that can connect us to other dimensions and aspects of our consciousness. In hyperdimensional dreamwork:

Astral Projection and Lucid Dreaming: Dreams can be gateways to astral projection or lucid dreaming, where one becomes consciously aware and can explore the astral plane or other dimensions with intention.

Symbolic and Literal Dimensions: Some dreams may be symbolic, offering insights and guidance through metaphors and symbols. Others might be literal experiences in different dimensions, providing direct experiences of other realities.

Temporal Fluidity: Dreams are not bound by linear time and can provide experiences of past, present, future, or parallel timelines.

Practices for Effective Dimensional Dreamwork

Engaging in dimensional dreamwork involves several practices and attitudes:

Dream Journaling: Keeping a dream journal helps in remembering and decoding the rich tapestry of dream experiences. Writing down dreams first thing in the morning preserves the details that are often quickly forgotten.

Intention Setting: Before sleeping, setting an intention or asking a specific question can direct the dream consciousness towards specific experiences or insights.

Meditation and Visualization: Techniques such as meditation and visualization before sleep can prepare the mind and spirit for deep, insightful dream experiences.

Roles and Benefits of Dimensional Dreamwork

Dimensional dreamwork serves multiple roles in the journey of a starseed and any individual exploring multidimensional realities:

Guidance and Insight: Dreams can provide guidance, offering solutions to problems or insights into complex life situations and spiritual questions.

Healing and Integration: Dreams often play a role in the healing process, helping to integrate different aspects of the self and work through emotional or spiritual issues.

Connection with Higher Selves and Guides: Dreams can facilitate communication with higher aspects of oneself, spirit guides, or other entities, offering wisdom and knowledge.

Navigating Challenges in Dimensional Dreamwork

Dimensional dreamwork, while enriching, also comes with challenges that need to be navigated:

Interpreting Dreams: The biggest challenge is often interpreting the dream correctly, distinguishing between literal and symbolic messages.

Fear and Control: Some dreams may evoke fear or confusion. Learning to maintain control and discernment in the dream state is crucial.

Integration into Waking Life: Integrating the insights and experiences from dreams into waking life in a meaningful way can be challenging but is essential for growth and understanding.

Dimensional dreamwork is a powerful tool for exploring the depths of consciousness and the myriad dimensions of existence. Through practices like dream journaling, intention setting, and meditation, individuals can harness the power of their dreams to gain insights, experience healing, and connect with higher aspects of themselves and the universe. As with all aspects of hyperdimensional existence, approaching dreamwork with respect, openness, and a willingness to learn and grow ensures a rich and rewarding journey.

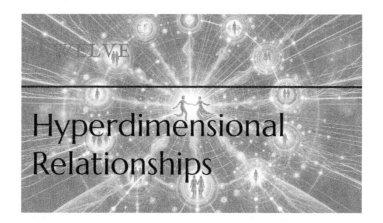

Soul Contracts Across Dimensions

The Concept of Soul Contracts

Soul contracts are agreements made at the soul level, often before birth, that shape our lives, relationships, and spiritual journey. These contracts are not rigid destinies but rather dynamic agreements intended to foster growth and evolution. In the context of hyperdimensional realities, soul contracts extend beyond our three-dimensional existence, involving various dimensions and lifetimes, and play a crucial role in our multidimensional evolution.

Understanding Multidimensional Soul Contracts

Soul contracts in a hyperdimensional framework involve multiple layers and implications:

Karmic Ties and Lessons: Many soul contracts are formed to address karmic debts or lessons from past lives. They provide opportunities for healing, learning, and balancing past actions across different dimensions.

Guidance and Growth: Soul contracts often bring individuals together to facilitate mutual growth. These relationships might challenge us but ultimately lead to profound personal and spiritual development.

Dimensional Intersection: Some contracts involve interactions with beings from other dimensions, allowing for the exchange of knowledge and energy that aids in the collective evolution of consciousness.

Identifying and Working with Soul Contracts

Working effectively with soul contracts involves recognition, understanding, and, at times, renegotiation or release:

Recognition and Awareness: The first step is recognizing the existence of soul contracts. This awareness often comes through introspection, meditation, or guidance from spiritual practices.

Learning from Relationships and Experiences: Understanding the deeper purpose behind life's challenges and relationships helps in identifying the lessons and growth opportunities presented by soul contracts.

Renegotiation and Release: Not all soul contracts are meant to last a lifetime. Some may be renegotiated or released, especially if they no longer serve the highest good or growth of the individuals involved.

The Role of Soul Contracts in Starseeds' Missions

For starseeds, soul contracts play a significant role in their missions on Earth:

Alignment with Mission: Many starseeds have soul contracts that align them with their purpose and missions in this lifetime, guiding them towards people and experiences that facilitate their work.

Healing and Activation: Soul contracts often involve healing both personal and ancestral wounds, which is crucial for activating higher potentials and abilities in starseeds.

Galactic and Earthly Connections: Starseeds may have contracts that involve connections with beings from their star origins and with humans, helping to bridge galactic wisdom and Earthly experiences.

Challenges and Growth Opportunities

Working with soul contracts is not without its challenges:

Difficult Relationships and Situations: Soul contracts can involve difficult relationships or challenging situations that are meant to push us towards growth but can be hard to navigate.

Misunderstanding the Contract: Misinterpreting the purpose and lessons of a soul contract can lead to repeated patterns and missed growth opportunities.

Balancing Free Will and Destiny: While soul contracts guide our paths, exercising free will and making conscious choices are essential for our growth and fulfillment.

Soul contracts are integral to understanding our journey through the multidimensional universe. They shape our experiences, relationships, and spiritual growth, extending beyond our current lifetime and dimension. For starseeds and those on a spiritual path, recognizing and working with these contracts is crucial for fulfilling their missions and evolving both personally and collectively. By embracing the lessons and opportunities presented by soul contracts, we navigate our hyperdimensional journey with greater purpose and clarity.

Twin Flames and Multidimensionality

The Twin Flame Connection

In the journey of the soul across dimensions, the concept of twin flames stands out as a profound and often misunderstood phenomenon. Twin flames are two halves of the same soul, created together and bound across time and space, destined to meet and unite. This connection transcends physicality, existing in the higher dimensions of consciousness and profoundly impacting the spiritual evolution of each individual.

Understanding the Multidimensional Nature of Twin Flames

The twin flame relationship is not limited to the physical dimension but spans across multiple realms of existence:

Energetic Resonance: Twin flames resonate at the same frequency, sharing a unique energetic signature. This connection is felt as an intense, inexplicable pull towards each other, transcending physical distance and circumstances.

Spiritual Growth and Evolution: The primary purpose of twin flame unions is to catalyze spiritual growth and evolution. These relationships often trigger deep healing, bringing to the surface unresolved issues and karmic patterns for resolution.

Dimensional Harmonization: Twin flames play a role in harmonizing energies across dimensions, their union contributing to the balance and ascension of the collective consciousness.

Navigating the Twin Flame Journey

The path of twin flames can be intense and challenging, requiring understanding and conscious effort to navigate:

Recognition and Acknowledgment: Recognizing the twin flame connection involves intuition and inner knowing. It often comes with a sense of familiarity and deep recognition that transcends logical understanding.

Healing and Personal Growth: Twin flame relationships illuminate personal weaknesses and unresolved issues, requiring both individuals to engage in self-healing and growth.

Unconditional Love and Release: The journey often involves learning lessons of unconditional love, forgiveness, and sometimes, the strength to let go, understanding that the connection goes beyond physical union.

The Role of Twin Flames in Starseeds' Missions

For starseeds, the twin flame connection holds particular significance in their missions on Earth:

Accelerated Awakening: Meeting a twin flame can accelerate the awakening process, propelling starseeds towards their spiritual mission with increased clarity and urgency.

Galactic and Earthly Missions: Twin flames often come together to fulfill joint missions that involve healing, teaching, or raising the consciousness of humanity and contributing to Earth's transition into higher dimensions.

Template for Unity Consciousness: Twin flame unions act as a template for unity consciousness, demonstrating the power of unconditional love and the interconnectedness of all beings.

Challenges and Transformative Potentials

Twin flame relationships are not without their challenges:

Intensity of the Connection: The intensity of the twin flame connection can be overwhelming, bringing turbulent emotions and deep-seated fears to the surface.

Separation and Reunion Cycles: Many twin flames experience cycles of separation and reunion, each phase offering lessons and opportunities for individual growth.

Misunderstanding and Idealization: There's often a tendency to idealize the twin flame connection, expecting it to be a perfect union, which can lead to disappointment and misunderstanding the true purpose of the relationship.

The twin flame connection is a powerful and transformative experience, deeply embedded in the fabric of multidimensional reality. For starseeds and those on a spiritual path, this connection offers profound opportunities for personal growth, spiritual awakening, and fulfilling their higher missions. Understanding and navigating the complexities of this relationship requires inner work, a deep commitment to personal growth, and an understanding of the higher purpose behind this profound union.

Soul Groups and Collective Consciousness

The Concept of Soul Groups

Soul groups represent clusters of souls who are interconnected through their energy frequencies and intentions, often sharing similar evolutionary paths and purposes. In the expansive realm of hyperdimensional realities, soul groups are more than mere associations; they are intricate networks of souls who incarnate together, supporting and facilitating each other's spiritual growth across multiple dimensions and lifetimes.

Dynamics of Soul Groups in Multidimensional Realities

In the vast landscape of existence, soul groups play a pivotal role in the evolution of consciousness:

Interdimensional Connections: Members of a soul group are connected not just in the physical realm but across various dimensions, often working together in different capacities, be it as guides, teachers, or companions.

Collective Missions: Many soul groups incarnate with specific collective missions that contribute to the greater good, such as raising the planet's vibration, healing ancestral wounds, or bringing about societal changes.

Karmic and Dharmic Bonds: The interactions within a soul group are governed by both karmic (past actions' consequences) and dharmic (purposeful and righteous) principles, facilitating learning and growth for each soul involved.

Recognizing and Connecting with Your Soul Group

Identifying and harmonizing with one's soul group can be a transformative experience:

Intuitive Recognition: Often, meeting a member of your soul group feels like a 'homecoming' – a deep, inexplicable sense of familiarity and comfort.

Synchronous Events: Encounters with soul group members are often marked by synchronicities or meaningful coincidences that guide these meetings.

Shared Vision and Values: There is usually a profound alignment in terms of spiritual values, visions, and aspirations among the members of a soul group.

The Impact of Soul Groups on Individual and Collective Growth

The influence of soul groups extends far beyond individual relationships, impacting the collective evolution:

Spiritual Awakening and Empowerment: Interaction within a soul group can trigger spiritual awakenings, empowering individuals to discover and fulfill their true potential and mission.

Healing and Support: Soul groups provide a support system for deep emotional and spiritual healing, offering unconditional love, understanding, and acceptance.

Galactic and Universal Contributions: The work done by soul groups often has ripple effects across galaxies and dimensions, contributing to the universal ascension process.

Challenges and Lessons in Soul Group Dynamics

Navigating soul group connections comes with its unique challenges:

Intense Relationships: Relationships within a soul group can be intense and challenging, as they often bring up unresolved issues for healing and growth.

Misaligned Expectations: There can be a tendency to have unrealistic expectations from soul group members, forgetting that each soul is on its unique journey of growth.

Balancing Individuality with Collectivity: While being part of a soul group, maintaining one's individuality and personal spiritual path is crucial.

Soul groups play an indispensable role in the grand scheme of hyperdimensional existence. They are not just gatherings of souls with shared intentions but vital cogs in the machinery of cosmic evolution, facilitating personal growth, collective ascension, and the fulfillment of higher universal plans. Recognizing and embracing one's place within a soul group offers profound insights and opportunities for evolution, both as individuals and as integral parts of the collective consciousness.

Dimensional Compatibility in Relationships

Navigating Relationships Across Dimensions

In the journey of a hyperdimensional existence, relationships take on a complex and multifaceted nature. Understanding dimensional compatibility involves recognizing how different individuals align or contrast in their vibrational frequencies, life missions, and soul evolution across various dimensions. This compatibility is not just about harmonizing in the physical realm but also about aligning on spiritual, emotional, and multidimensional levels.

The Dynamics of Dimensional Compatibility

Vibrational Resonance: At the core of dimensional compatibility is the concept of vibrational resonance. Relationships thrive when individuals resonate at similar frequencies, sharing similar values, goals, and spiritual understandings.

Soul Evolution and Life Missions: Compatibility extends to the alignment of life missions and stages of soul evolution.

Partners who are on similar paths or who complement each other's growth journeys tend to have stronger, more meaningful connections.

Multidimensional Synergy: True compatibility in relationships in a hyperdimensional context means that the connection is beneficial and harmonious across various dimensions of existence, enhancing each other's journey towards spiritual growth and fulfillment.

Identifying and Cultivating Dimensional Compatibility

Intuitive Recognition: Often, dimensional compatibility is recognized through an intuitive feeling of deep connection and understanding, going beyond surface-level interactions.

Communication and Shared Growth: Open communication about spiritual beliefs, life goals, and personal growth is essential. Relationships that encourage mutual growth and exploration of multidimensional aspects tend to be more compatible.

Energy Work and Spiritual Practices: Engaging in joint energy work, meditation, or other spiritual practices can enhance compatibility, creating a shared vibrational space that transcends physical limitations.

Challenges and Opportunities in Multidimensional Relationships

Navigating Differences: Differences in vibrational frequencies or stages of spiritual evolution can pose challenges. These differences, however, also offer opportunities for learning and growth.

Maintaining Individual Paths: It's important to balance the shared journey with individual paths. Each person must honor their unique journey and growth process within the relationship.

Transcending Physical Limitations: In some cases, relationships may exist more strongly on the spiritual or energetic level than in the physical realm. Recognizing and valuing these connections is crucial in a hyperdimensional context.

The Role of Relationships in Hyperdimensional Growth

Catalysts for Evolution: Relationships in a hyperdimensional reality often act as catalysts for spiritual and personal evolution, pushing individuals to confront their shadows, heal past traumas, and advance on their spiritual path.

Galactic and Universal Harmony: These relationships play a role in the larger cosmic scheme, contributing to the balance and harmony of energies across dimensions and, ultimately, to the ascension process of the collective consciousness.

Expanding Consciousness: Through relationships, individuals are often able to access and explore different facets of their consciousness and experience profound growth that transcends the physical dimension.

Dimensional compatibility in relationships is a complex and deeply enriching aspect of hyperdimensional existence. It involves not only harmonizing in the physical world but also aligning across various dimensions of being. These relationships, marked by vibrational resonance, shared missions, and mutual growth, play a significant role in the spiritual evolution of the individuals involved and the collective consciousness. Navigating these connections with awareness, openness, and a commitment to growth can lead to profound transformations and a deeper understanding of the interconnectedness of all existence.

The Cosmic Family Tree

Understanding the Cosmic Family Tree

The concept of the Cosmic Family Tree extends beyond the traditional understanding of family lineage, encompassing a vast network of connections that transcend time, space, and dimensions. In the hyperdimensional framework, this tree represents the intricate web of soul connections, lineages, and relationships that form the fabric of the cosmos. Each being, each soul, is a vital part of this cosmic tapestry, interconnected through the threads of universal consciousness.

Branches of the Cosmic Family Tree

Soul Lineages: At the heart of the Cosmic Family Tree are soul lineages - groups of souls emanating from the same source or oversoul. These lineages represent deep spiritual connections, shared missions, and collective evolution across various dimensions and incarnations.

Starseed Connections: For starseeds, the Cosmic Family Tree includes connections to their star systems of origin, such as the Pleiades, Sirius, Arcturus, and others. These connections influence their missions on Earth, providing them with unique abilities, perspectives, and purposes.

Intergalactic Alliances: The tree also represents alliances and relationships formed across galaxies and dimensions, encompassing a wide array of beings, from celestial entities to interdimensional guides.

Navigating the Cosmic Family Tree

Understanding and navigating one's position in the Cosmic Family Tree involves several key aspects:

Akashic Records Exploration: Accessing the Akashic Records, the universal database of all experiences, can provide insights into one's soul lineage and connections within the Cosmic Family Tree.

Intuitive Recognition and Remembrance: Often, connections to the Cosmic Family Tree are felt intuitively. Moments of remembrance may occur during meditation, dream work, or through synchronistic encounters.

Spiritual Practices and Guidance: Engaging in spiritual practices and seeking guidance from mentors or spiritual guides can facilitate deeper understanding and integration of these cosmic connections.

Roles and Responsibilities within the Cosmic Family Tree

Being part of this vast cosmic network carries roles and responsibilities:

Spiritual Evolution: Each soul contributes to the evolution of the entire Cosmic Family Tree through its growth, experiences, and ascension process.

Galactic Service and Earth's Ascension: Many beings within the tree are actively involved in assisting Earth's transition into higher consciousness, playing roles as healers, teachers, and lightworkers.

Universal Harmony and Balance: The interactions and growth within the Cosmic Family Tree contribute to the harmony and balance of the universe, reflecting the interconnected nature of all existence.

Challenges and Growth Opportunities

Engaging with the Cosmic Family Tree is not without its challenges:

Complexity of Connections: The sheer complexity and depth of connections can be overwhelming, requiring discernment and gradual integration.

Past Life Resonances and Karmic Patterns: Connections within the tree may bring up past life memories or unresolved karmic patterns that need healing.

Balancing Earthly and Cosmic Identities: Navigating one's role in the Cosmic Family Tree while fulfilling earthly responsibilities can be challenging, requiring a balance between spiritual and mundane aspects of life.

The Cosmic Family Tree is a profound and expansive concept that offers a deeper understanding of our place in the cosmos. It reveals the interconnectedness of all souls, lineages, and galactic alliances, emphasizing the unity and collective evolution of all beings. Navigating this cosmic network enriches our spiritual journey, offering insights into our roles, responsibilities, and connections across the vast universe. As we explore and integrate our place within this tree, we contribute to the greater tapestry of universal consciousness and the ascension of the collective.

Thirteen
Challenges and Solutions

Navigating Dimensional Shift Symptoms

Understanding Dimensional Shifts

Dimensional shifts refer to the transitions and changes experienced as one navigates through different frequencies and dimensions of consciousness. These shifts are not just metaphysical concepts but real experiences that can have profound physical, emotional, and spiritual effects. For starseeds and those sensitive to energy fluctuations, understanding and navigating these symptoms is a crucial part of their hyperdimensional journey.

Recognizing Symptoms of Dimensional Shifts

Dimensional shifts can manifest in various ways, often resembling physical or psychological symptoms:

Physical Symptoms: These may include unusual fatigue, changes in sleep patterns, physical sensations like ringing in the ears, or even temporary disorientation. These symptoms occur as the body adjusts to different energetic frequencies.

Emotional Fluctuations: Individuals might experience intense, unexplained emotional highs and lows, or a sense of emotional detachment. This is often due to the clearing of old emotional patterns and the integration of higher vibrational energies.

Changes in Perception and Awareness: Enhanced intuition, altered states of consciousness, or sudden insights and realizations can occur as one's awareness expands into higher dimensions.

Managing and Easing Symptoms

Navigating these symptoms effectively involves several strategies:

Grounding Techniques: Engaging in grounding practices such as meditation, spending time in nature, or physical activities can help maintain balance and stability during these shifts.

Self-Care and Rest: Listening to the body's needs, ensuring adequate rest, and engaging in nurturing activities can help manage physical and emotional symptoms.

Spiritual Practices: Maintaining a regular spiritual practice provides a stable foundation and enhances one's ability to integrate these new energies harmoniously.

Growth Opportunities and Challenges

Dimensional shifts, while challenging, offer significant opportunities for growth:

Personal and Spiritual Evolution: These shifts are catalysts for profound personal and spiritual growth, leading to expanded consciousness, increased intuition, and a deeper understanding of one's true self.

Release of Old Patterns: Dimensional shifts often initiate the release of old patterns, beliefs, and emotional blockages, facilitating healing and transformation.

Enhanced Multidimensional Awareness: As one navigates through these shifts, they often develop an enhanced perception of multidimensional realities, deepening their connection to the higher aspects of their being.

Integration and Harmonization

Successfully integrating these experiences is key:

Embracing Change: Accepting and embracing the changes occurring within and around oneself is essential for a smooth transition.

Seeking Support and Guidance: Connecting with like-minded individuals or seeking guidance from spiritual mentors can provide support and insights during these times.

Continuous Learning and Adaptation: Staying open to learning and adapting to new experiences and understandings helps in harmonizing with these energetic shifts.

Navigating dimensional shift symptoms is a vital aspect of living a hyperdimensional life. These shifts, while sometimes disconcerting, are integral to the evolutionary process, facilitating personal and collective growth. By managing these symptoms with care, understanding their purpose, and integrating the lessons they bring, individuals can move through these transitions with grace and ease, stepping into a more expanded and aware state of being.

Overcoming Multidimensional Fatigue

Understanding Multidimensional Fatigue

Multidimensional fatigue is a state often experienced by starseeds and those deeply engaged in spiritual and energetic work across multiple dimensions. Unlike regular physical tiredness, this type of fatigue encompasses emotional, spiritual, and energetic aspects. It arises from the intense demands of navigating various frequencies and realms, processing cosmic energies, and often, the challenges of grounding these experiences in the physical world.

Symptoms and Causes of Multidimensional Fatigue

Symptoms: It manifests as a deep sense of exhaustion that rest or sleep cannot easily alleviate. It may be accompanied by a feeling of disconnection, emotional numbness, or a temporary loss of spiritual purpose and direction.

Causes: The causes are diverse, including energy overextension, constant shifting between different vibrations, healing work, or processing large amounts of cosmic information and light codes.

Strategies for Managing Multidimensional Fatigue

To effectively manage and overcome multidimensional fatigue, several strategies can be employed:

Energetic Hygiene: Regular energy clearing practices, such as grounding, cleansing one's aura, and protective visualization, help maintain energetic integrity.

Balanced Lifestyle: Incorporating a balanced lifestyle with adequate physical rest, nutrition, and leisure is essential. It's important to allow the physical body to recuperate.

Mindful Engagement: Being mindful of one's energy levels and not overcommitting to energetic work helps prevent burnout. Learning to say no and setting energetic boundaries is crucial.

The Role of Rest and Integration

Rest: Allowing time for rest and disengagement from energetic activities is not a sign of weakness but a necessary phase for rejuvenation and sustaining one's spiritual journey.

Integration: Periods of rest provide an opportunity for the integration of experiences and energies encountered in different dimensions. This integration is essential for personal growth and clarity.

Connecting with Nature and Elemental Energies

Nature's Healing: Spending time in nature is a powerful way to recharge and realign with Earth's natural frequencies. Natural settings provide a harmonious energy that soothes and rejuvenates.

Elemental Connection: Connecting with elemental energies – Earth, Water, Air, Fire – can help restore balance and vitality.

Each element offers unique healing properties and can be a source of strength and renewal.

Seeking Support and Community Connection

Community Support: Sharing experiences with like-minded individuals or communities provides emotional support and valuable insights, reminding one that they are not alone in their journey.

Professional Guidance: Sometimes, seeking guidance from spiritual mentors, healers, or therapists who understand the nature of multidimensional work can provide relief and strategies for coping.

Personal Spiritual Practice and Self-Compassion

Spiritual Practice: Maintaining a personal spiritual practice tailored to one's needs and energy levels helps in staying grounded and connected to one's core essence.

Self-Compassion: Practicing self-compassion and kindness, acknowledging the challenges of multidimensional existence, and honoring one's journey is vital for emotional and spiritual well-being.

Overcoming multidimensional fatigue is a crucial aspect of the hyperdimensional journey, especially for starseeds and spiritual workers deeply involved in the energetic transformation of themselves and the planet. Recognizing the signs, understanding the causes, and employing effective management strategies are essential steps in maintaining vitality and continuing on this profound path. By embracing rest, integration, nature's healing, community support, and personal spiritual practices, individuals can navigate this journey with greater ease and resilience, continuing to contribute to the collective ascension process.

Psychic Protections and Energy Shields

The Need for Psychic Protection

In the realm of hyperdimensional existence, the concept of psychic protection becomes paramount. As individuals navigate through various dimensions and interact with a multitude of energies, they become more susceptible to energetic influences that can impact their physical, emotional, and spiritual well-being. Psychic protection involves techniques and practices that safeguard an individual's energy field from negative influences and maintain energetic integrity.

Fundamental Techniques for Psychic Protection

Shielding Techniques: This involves visualizing a protective barrier around oneself, often imagined as a sphere of light or a mirrored surface that deflects negative energies. This practice can be reinforced daily, especially before engaging in spiritual work or entering energetically dense environments.

Grounding Practices: Grounding helps anchor one's energy to the Earth, providing stability and resilience against external energies. Techniques include walking barefoot on the ground, meditation focused on connecting with Earth, and visualizing roots extending from one's feet into the ground.

Cleansing Rituals: Regularly cleansing one's personal space, aura, and energy tools (like crystals) is crucial. This can be done using sage smudging, sound vibrations (like bells or singing bowls), or energy clearing visualizations.

Advanced Psychic Protection Strategies

Use of Crystals and Talismans: Certain crystals, like black tourmaline, amethyst, and selenite, are known for their protective properties. Wearing these crystals or having them in one's environment can provide an additional layer of psychic defense.

Protective Mantras and Affirmations: Reciting mantras or affirmations that affirm one's safety and energetic sovereignty can be a powerful tool for psychic protection.

Collaboration with Spiritual Guides: Requesting protection from one's spiritual guides or guardian angels can provide a significant shield in the higher dimensions.

Balancing Protection with Openness

While psychic protection is essential, it is equally important to maintain a balance and not close oneself off from positive experiences and energies:

Discernment: Developing discernment to recognize what needs protection and what can be openly embraced is crucial in the journey of spiritual growth.

Fear vs. Awareness: Psychic protection should come from a place of awareness and care, not fear. Operating from fear can create a barrier to positive experiences and spiritual connections.

Regular Review and Adaptation: As one grows spiritually, their protection needs may change. Regularly reviewing and adapting one's protective practices ensures they remain effective and aligned with one's spiritual journey.

Integration into Daily Life

Incorporating psychic protection into daily life should be seamless and natural:

Routine Practices: Integrating simple practices like shielding and grounding into daily routines ensures continuous protection.

Mindful Interactions: Being mindful of the energies one interacts with, whether through people, places, or digital mediums, can help in maintaining energetic hygiene.

Educational Empowerment: Continually educating oneself about psychic protection and energy work empowers individuals to take proactive steps in managing their energetic health.

Psychic protection and the use of energy shields are crucial components of living a hyperdimensional life. They empower individuals to navigate through various dimensions safely and effectively, maintaining their energetic integrity and supporting their spiritual evolution. By incorporating these practices into daily life, one can ensure a balanced approach to protection, openness, and growth, enhancing their journey across the multiple realities of existence.

Dark Night of the Soul in Hyperdimensionality

Exploring the Dark Night of the Soul

The Dark Night of the Soul is a profound, deeply transformative phase often encountered on the spiritual journey, particularly within the context of hyperdimensionality. It is characterized by a sense of spiritual desolation, loss of meaning, and an intense grappling with the deeper aspects of the soul. This phase, while challenging, is crucial for profound spiritual growth and awakening.

Characteristics of the Dark Night in Hyperdimensional Context

Intense Emotional Turbulence: Individuals may experience profound sadness, loneliness, or despair, feeling disconnected from their spiritual source and purpose.

Questioning and Doubt: Deep existential questions arise, leading to doubts about one's beliefs, path, and even the nature of reality itself.

Shifts in Perception: The Dark Night often brings about a dismantling of previous perceptions and understandings, making way for new insights and higher levels of consciousness.

Navigating the Dark Night

Successfully navigating the Dark Night of the Soul requires resilience, patience, and a deep trust in the process:

Acceptance and Surrender: Accepting this phase as a natural part of the spiritual journey and surrendering to the process can alleviate resistance and open pathways for growth.

Seeking Support: Engaging with spiritual mentors, counselors, or supportive communities can provide guidance and reassurance during this challenging time.

Maintaining Spiritual Practices: Continuing with meditation, prayer, or other spiritual practices, even when they seem futile, can provide a lifeline through the darkness.

Transformation and Renewal

The Dark Night of the Soul, despite its difficulties, is a gateway to profound transformation:

Emergence of a Deeper Understanding: As one emerges from this phase, they often gain deeper spiritual insights, a more authentic connection with their true self, and a renewed sense of purpose.

Increased Empathy and Compassion: Having traversed the depths of despair, individuals often develop greater empathy and compassion for others' suffering.

Enhanced Multidimensional Awareness: This phase can lead to an enhanced perception of multidimensional realities, providing a richer, more nuanced understanding of the universe.

Integration and Moving Forward

Post Dark Night, integrating the experiences and lessons learned is crucial:

Reflective Contemplation: Taking time to reflect on the journey and its revelations can help integrate these insights into one's life and spiritual practice.

Gradual Re-engagement: Slowly re-engaging with daily life, while incorporating new understandings, helps in grounding the transformation experienced.

Sharing Insights and Experiences: Sharing one's journey through the Dark Night can assist others on their path and reinforce one's own learning.

The Role of the Dark Night in Hyperdimensional Existence

In the broader context of hyperdimensional existence, the Dark Night plays a significant role:

Catalyst for Ascension: It acts as a catalyst for ascension to higher states of consciousness, clearing old patterns and raising vibrational frequencies.

Balance and Integration: It helps in balancing and integrating the various dimensional aspects of one's being, leading to a more holistic and unified existence.

Galactic and Universal Contribution: The personal transformation achieved contributes to the collective evolution of consciousness across dimensions.

The Dark Night of the Soul is a critical and transformative phase in the journey of hyperdimensional existence. While challenging, it is a profound process of purification, introspection, and spiritual renewal, leading to greater wisdom, empathy, and an enhanced understanding of the multidimensional nature of reality. Embracing this phase with acceptance, patience, and trust paves the way for significant spiritual growth and a deeper alignment with one's true purpose in the cosmic tapestry.

Navigating Cosmic Tests and Challenges

Understanding Cosmic Tests

In the journey of hyperdimensional existence, starseeds and spiritually aware individuals often encounter what can be referred to as cosmic tests. These are challenges or situations that arise, not as mere coincidences, but as orchestrated experiences meant to catalyze growth, learning, and spiritual advancement. These tests often push individuals to their limits, compelling them to harness inner strengths and gain deeper insights into their multidimensional nature.

Recognizing Cosmic Tests

Recurring Themes: Often, cosmic tests present themselves as recurring themes or patterns in one's life. These can manifest as repeated obstacles, similar types of relationships, or persistent issues, signaling unresolved lessons or karma.

Intensified Emotions: Cosmic tests can evoke intense emotions or reactions, sometimes disproportionate to the situation at hand. This intensity is a sign of deeper underlying issues coming to the surface for resolution.

Synchronicities and Signs: The universe often communicates through synchronicities and signs, guiding and providing insights into the nature of the tests being faced.

Strategies for Navigating Cosmic Tests

Successfully navigating cosmic tests involves a multifaceted approach:

Mindfulness and Awareness: Staying present and mindful allows one to recognize the lessons embedded in each situation. Awareness brings clarity and reduces the likelihood of reacting impulsively.

Emotional and Spiritual Processing: Embracing emotional and spiritual processing, including meditation, journaling, or therapy, can help in understanding and integrating the lessons of these tests.

Seeking Higher Guidance: Turning to spiritual guides, mentors, or one's higher self for guidance and clarity can provide valuable insights and support.

Growth and Evolution Through Cosmic Tests

Cosmic tests, while challenging, are integral to spiritual evolution:

Personal Growth: Each test brings an opportunity for personal growth, helping individuals to transcend limitations and embrace their higher potential.

Karmic Resolution: Successfully navigating these tests often leads to the resolution of karmic cycles, allowing for advancement in one's spiritual journey.

Enhanced Multidimensional Awareness: Through these challenges, individuals gain a deeper understanding of the interconnectedness of all dimensions and their role in the cosmic scheme.

Integrating the Lessons

Post-test integration is crucial for holistic growth:

Reflection and Contemplation: Taking time to reflect on the experiences and insights gained is key to integrating the lessons learned.

Sharing and Teaching: Sharing one's experiences and lessons with others can not only help in solidifying one's own understanding but also assist others in their journeys.

Continued Openness to Learning: Remaining open to continuous learning and being receptive to new challenges ensures ongoing spiritual development and readiness for higher ascension.

Cosmic Tests in the Collective Context

Cosmic tests also play a role in the collective evolution of consciousness:

Collective Learning: The lessons learned by individuals contribute to the collective wisdom and evolution of humanity and beyond.

Energetic Contributions: Successfully navigating these tests contributes positively to the collective energy field, aiding in the ascension process of the planet and the universe.

Galactic and Universal Harmony: Each individual's growth through cosmic tests plays a part in maintaining the balance and harmony of the cosmos, reflecting the interconnected nature of all existence.

Navigating cosmic tests and challenges is an essential aspect of living a hyperdimensional life. These tests serve as catalysts for personal and collective growth, pushing individuals to delve deeper into their spiritual essence and fulfill their cosmic missions. By embracing these challenges with mindfulness, emotional and spiritual processing, and seeking higher guidance, one can transcend limitations and contribute to the greater evolutionary process of the universe.

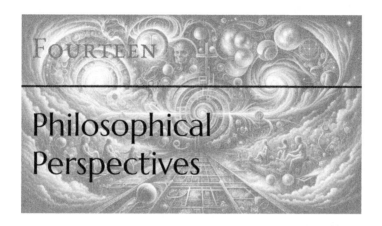

Philosophical Perspectives

Quantum Mechanics and Spirituality

The Intersection of Science and Spirituality

Quantum mechanics, a fundamental theory in physics, has intriguing parallels with spirituality, especially in the realm of hyperdimensional existence. Let's delve into how quantum theory not only aligns with but also enriches spiritual understanding, offering a more holistic view of the universe and our place within it.

Quantum Theory and Consciousness

Quantum mechanics has revolutionized our understanding of the microscopic world, revealing that at the subatomic level, particles behave in ways that defy classical physics. This theory introduces concepts like the wave-particle duality and quantum entanglement, which resonate with spiritual teachings about the interconnectedness of all things and the non-linear nature of reality.

Wave-Particle Duality: This principle suggests that subatomic particles exhibit both particle-like and wave-like properties. In a spiritual context, this duality reflects the idea that reality is not fixed but is influenced by consciousness and perception.

Quantum Entanglement: Entanglement posits that particles can become correlated in such a way that the state of one instantaneously influences the state of another, regardless of distance. This phenomenon echoes spiritual notions of oneness and the interconnected web of life, where actions in one part of the universe can affect another.

Quantum Mechanics and Multidimensional Existence

In hyperdimensional understanding, quantum mechanics offers a framework for comprehending the existence of multiple dimensions and realities:

Superposition: The concept of superposition, where particles can exist in multiple states simultaneously until observed, parallels the idea of multiple dimensions or realities co-existing until one is experienced or chosen.

Observer Effect: The observer effect in quantum mechanics, where the act of observation affects the system being observed, aligns with the concept that consciousness shapes reality, a core principle in many spiritual traditions.

Implications for Spiritual Practices

Quantum mechanics can deepen spiritual practices by providing a scientific basis for phenomena often regarded as purely metaphysical:

Manifestation and Intention: The understanding that consciousness can influence physical reality supports spiritual practices like manifestation and the power of intention.

Energy Healing: Quantum theory suggests that everything is energy, resonating with the idea that energy healing can affect physical and emotional well-being.

Meditation and Mindfulness: Quantum mechanics underscores the importance of the observer's mindset, aligning with practices that cultivate mindfulness and a focused, intentional state of consciousness.

Bridging the Gap Between Science and Spirituality

Quantum mechanics serves as a bridge between science and spirituality, offering a common language and understanding:

Unified Worldview: It supports a more integrated worldview where science and spirituality are not at odds but are complementary ways of understanding the universe.

Expanding Consciousness: This integration encourages an expansion of consciousness, moving beyond materialistic views to embrace a more holistic understanding of existence.

Collective Evolution: The merging of quantum physics and spirituality can catalyze a collective evolution, fostering a deeper appreciation for the mystery and interconnectedness of life.

The relationship between quantum mechanics and spirituality provides a profound and compelling framework for exploring hyperdimensional existence. It bridges the often-perceived gap between science and spirituality, offering a more enriched, cohesive understanding of the universe. By embracing the principles of quantum theory in spiritual practices and perspectives, individuals can deepen their awareness of the interconnected nature of all things and their role in the cosmic tapestry. This synthesis not only enhances personal spiritual growth but also contributes to the collective evolution of consciousness.

Free Will vs. Destiny in Multiple Realities

The Intricate Dance of Free Will and Destiny

In the realms of hyperdimensional existence, the interplay between free will and destiny forms a complex, yet harmonious dance. Let's investigate how these concepts operate within the framework of multiple dimensions, influencing the journey of Starseeds and shaping the fabric of their experiences.

Understanding Free Will in Hyperdimensions

Concept of Free Will: Free will represents the capacity to make choices independently, a cornerstone of individual empowerment and self-determination. In hyperdimensional contexts, it allows beings to navigate their own paths across different dimensions, each choice birthing new possibilities and realities.

The Power of Choice: Every decision made with free will carves out a unique trajectory in the cosmic tapestry. It's a powerful tool for shaping one's destiny, allowing Starseeds to explore, learn, and grow within the vast expanses of the multiverse.

Destiny's Role in Multiple Realities

Defining Destiny: Destiny, often perceived as a preordained path, is a series of potential outcomes in the hyperdimensional view, each influenced by choices made through free will. It is the overarching narrative of a soul's journey, encompassing various lifetimes and dimensions.

Predestined Encounters: While the broader strokes of destiny might be pre-scripted, the details of how one reaches these destiny points and the ensuing outcomes largely depend on free will.

Interplay and Coexistence

Navigating Timelines: Free will determines the course through different timelines, while destiny ensures the encounter with certain pivotal experiences designed for soul growth and evolution.

Soul Contracts and Life Plans: Before incarnating, souls may agree upon certain key experiences or lessons, indicative of destiny's framework. However, the manner and timing of these experiences are shaped by free will.

Harmonizing Free Will and Destiny

Conscious Choice Making: By attuning to their higher selves and intuition, Starseeds can make choices that harmonize their free will with their soul's destiny, leading to a balanced and fulfilling journey.

Destiny Points as Catalysts: Certain predestined events act as catalysts for significant growth and transformation, guiding Starseeds towards their ultimate purpose while respecting their free will.

In the hyperdimensional paradigm, free will and destiny are not opposing forces but complementary aspects of a greater cosmic dance. Understanding their dynamics is crucial for Starseeds navigating multiple realities. It's through this intricate interplay that they find their unique path to spiritual enlightenment and cosmic understanding. This journey, a blend of choice and destiny, is what shapes the essence of their hyperdimensional existence.

Duality and Polarity Across Dimensions

Understanding Duality in Hyperdimensional Realms

The concept of duality is deeply rooted in the fabric of hyperdimensional existence. It's a fundamental principle that manifests in various forms across multiple dimensions, offering Starseeds a unique perspective on the nature of reality.

The Essence of Duality

Yin and Yang of Existence: At its core, duality represents the coexistence of opposites—light and dark, positive and negative, physical and non-physical. These opposing forces are not conflicting but complementary, creating a harmonious balance in the universe.

Role in Evolution and Growth: Duality serves as a catalyst for growth and evolution. The contrasts and challenges it presents are opportunities for Starseeds to learn, adapt, and advance on their spiritual journey.

Polarity in Multidimensional Perspectives

Polarity is an extension of duality, seen in the varied expressions and experiences across different dimensions. It's the driving force behind the diverse experiences that Starseeds encounter in their multidimensional travels.

The Dynamics of Polarity

Manifestation in Dimensions: Polarity manifests differently in various dimensions. In higher dimensions, polarity might be subtle and more spiritually oriented, while in lower dimensions, it can be stark, manifesting as physical or material contrasts.

Balancing Polarities: Understanding and balancing these polarities is crucial for Starseeds. It involves recognizing the interconnectedness of all things and the purpose behind apparent contradictions.

Navigating Duality and Polarity

For Starseeds, navigating the realms of duality and polarity is an essential aspect of their journey. It's about understanding the deeper significance behind these concepts and using this knowledge for personal and collective growth.

Strategies for Harmonious Existence

Embracing Opposites: Accepting and embracing the opposite forces helps Starseeds to maintain equilibrium. It's about finding the middle path that acknowledges both sides of the spectrum.

Learning from Contrasts: Every experience, whether perceived as positive or negative, holds valuable lessons. Starseeds learn to use these experiences as stepping stones towards higher consciousness.

Duality and polarity in hyperdimensional realities are not merely concepts but lived experiences that shape the journey of every Starseed. By understanding and embracing these principles, Starseeds can navigate the complexities of multiple dimensions with wisdom and grace, turning challenges into opportunities for profound spiritual growth and evolution.

The Illusion of Separateness in Hyperdimensional Realities

Unraveling the Veil of Separation

The concept of separateness is a prevalent illusion in the physical realm, often leading individuals to feel disconnected from the larger cosmic whole. For Starseeds navigating hyperdimensional realities, understanding and transcending this illusion is vital for spiritual growth and fulfillment.

Exploring the Illusion

Perceived Isolation: In many dimensions, especially the physical, entities experience a sense of isolation, believing themselves to be distinct and separate from others and the universe. This perception is a fundamental aspect of the human experience but is not the ultimate truth.

Roots in Physical Reality: The illusion stems from the physical senses and the ego, which interprets reality through a lens of individuality and distinctiveness. This perspective, while necessary for survival and individual development, obscures the deeper truth of interconnectedness.

Transcending the Illusion

In hyperdimensional journeys, Starseeds encounter various states of consciousness that challenge the notion of separateness. These experiences are pivotal in understanding the interconnected nature of existence.

Pathways to Unity

Experiencing Oneness: Through meditation, astral projection, and other spiritual practices, Starseeds often experience a state of oneness with the universe. These experiences reveal the interconnected fabric of existence, where separation is merely an illusion.

Learning from Higher Dimensions: In higher dimensions, the sense of individuality is less pronounced. Entities in these realms often function with a collective consciousness, further illustrating the interconnectedness of all beings.

Practical Implications for Starseeds

The understanding of the illusion of separateness has profound implications for Starseeds in their mission on Earth and other realms.

Living with the Awareness of Oneness

Empathy and Compassion: Recognizing the interconnected nature of existence fosters a deeper sense of empathy and compassion. Starseeds, acknowledging their unity with others, are often driven to act for the greater good.

Holistic Approach to Life: With the awareness of interconnectedness, Starseeds approach life holistically, understanding that actions in one area can affect the whole. This perspective encourages sustainable and harmonious living.

The illusion of separateness, while a dominant aspect of physical existence, is merely a veil that obscures the deeper truth of interconnectedness and unity. For Starseeds, transcending this illusion is essential for spiritual evolution and the fulfillment of their cosmic missions. We have shed light on the importance of recognizing and overcoming the illusion of separateness, urging Starseeds to embrace the unity of all existence as they navigate the complex and multidimensional reality of their journeys. Through this understanding, Starseeds are empowered to live more compassionately and purposefully, contributing to the harmonious evolution of the universe.

The Nature of Evil in Multidimensional Perspectives

Unveiling the Multidimensional Concept of Evil

In the exploration of hyperdimensional realities, Starseeds confront the concept of evil, a notion that varies significantly across different dimensions and perspectives. Let's delve into the nature of evil as understood in a multidimensional context, offering insights into its origins, manifestations, and the lessons it offers.

Understanding Evil in Various Realms

Dimensional Variations: Evil, as perceived in the physical realm, often represents harm, suffering, or negative intentions. However, in higher dimensions, the concept of evil transcends simple moral judgments, becoming a complex interplay of energies and consciousness.

Role of Duality: In many dimensions, especially those close to the physical plane, evil is seen as a part of the duality of existence - a necessary contrast to good. This duality is less pronounced or even non-existent in higher dimensions.

Transcending the Dichotomy of Good and Evil

For Starseeds, transcending the binary view of good and evil is a significant step in their spiritual evolution. This process involves understanding the deeper implications of these concepts.

Beyond Moral Judgments

Evil as a Catalyst for Growth: In many instances, what is perceived as evil serves as a catalyst for spiritual growth and evolution. Challenges and negative experiences often lead to greater understanding and expansion of consciousness.

Balancing Energies: In higher dimensions, the concept of evil is often seen in terms of imbalanced energies rather than moral failings. Restoring balance is key to resolving these issues.

Practical Implications for Starseeds

The understanding of evil in a multidimensional context has profound implications for Starseeds in their earthly missions and spiritual journeys.

Navigating the Complexity of Evil

Compassionate Understanding: Recognizing the multifaceted nature of evil enables Starseeds to approach situations with compassion and understanding, rather than judgment.

Energy Work and Healing: By viewing evil as an imbalance, Starseeds can focus on healing and energy work to restore harmony, both within themselves and in the environments they interact with.

The nature of evil in a multidimensional context challenges the traditional understanding of morality and ethics. For Starseeds, comprehending this complex concept is essential for their growth and effectiveness in their missions. Recognizing that what is often labeled as evil may be a necessary part of the cosmic balance or a catalyst for growth, they can approach their tasks with greater wisdom and compassion. We have examined a nuanced perspective on the nature of evil, encouraging Starseeds to look beyond surface-level judgments and to see the deeper energetic and spiritual dynamics at play in the universe.

FIFTEEN
Starseed Activations and Upgrades

DNA Activations and Cosmic Downloads

Understanding DNA Activations

In the realm of hyperdimensional existence, DNA activations are pivotal moments for Starseeds, symbolizing significant shifts in their consciousness and physical being. These activations are not merely biological but are deeply intertwined with spiritual awakening and multidimensional awareness.

The Science of Spiritual DNA

Multidimensional DNA: Beyond the physical strands, DNA in hyperdimensional theory includes layers of energetic and spiritual elements that connect Starseeds to higher realms of existence.

Unlocking Latent Potentials: DNA activations trigger the unlocking of latent spiritual potentials, enhancing psychic abilities, and deepening the connection with universal consciousness.

Cosmic Downloads: Receiving Higher Knowledge

Cosmic downloads refer to the process where Starseeds receive bursts of information, energy, and awareness from higher dimensions. This often occurs during meditation, dream states, or moments of profound introspection.

Channels of Higher Wisdom

Intuitive Knowledge: Cosmic downloads often manifest as sudden insights, intuitive understanding, or creative inspiration, providing guidance and clarity on the Starseed's path.

Integration Challenges: Integrating this knowledge into daily life can be challenging, requiring a balance between earthly existence and higher dimensional realities.

Practical Implications for Starseeds

Understanding and harnessing the power of DNA activations and cosmic downloads is crucial for Starseeds in fulfilling their missions on Earth and beyond.

Navigating DNA Activations

Embracing Change: DNA activations can lead to profound personal changes. Embracing these changes with an open heart and mind is essential for growth.

Physical and Energetic Support: Supporting the physical body through healthy practices and energetic work is vital to handle these activations smoothly.

Maximizing Cosmic Downloads

Creating Receptive Spaces: Regular meditation and creating spaces of quiet and receptivity aid in receiving and understanding cosmic downloads.

Journaling and Reflection: Recording insights and reflecting on their meanings can help integrate these downloads into practical wisdom.

DNA activations and cosmic downloads are fundamental aspects of a Starseed's journey, offering gateways to higher wisdom and deeper understanding of their role in the universe. By embracing these experiences and learning to integrate their lessons, Starseeds can significantly advance on their paths, both spiritually and in their missions.

Receiving Light Codes

The Phenomenon of Light Codes

In the journey of a hyperdimensional Starseed, receiving light codes is a transformative experience. These codes are energetic patterns and frequencies that convey deep spiritual information. They are essential in the evolutionary process of consciousness, facilitating a profound connection with the higher dimensions.

Nature and Origin of Light Codes

Energetic Imprints: Light codes are seen as vibrational imprints that carry cosmic intelligence. They resonate with the multidimensional aspects of a Starseed's being.

Sources of Light Codes: These codes are believed to originate from various cosmic sources such as star systems, higher-dimensional entities, and the universal field of consciousness.

Integration and Activation of Light Codes

The process of integrating light codes involves a harmonization of these energies with the individual's physical and energetic systems. This integration can lead to significant changes in perception, heightened awareness, and the unlocking of latent spiritual abilities.

Key Aspects of Integration

Physical and Energetic Alignment: A balance in physical health and energetic practices like meditation and energy work is crucial for the smooth integration of light codes.

Emotional and Mental Readiness: Emotionally and mentally, a Starseed must be prepared to receive and process these high-frequency codes without resistance.

Practical Applications in Daily Life

Incorporating the knowledge and changes brought about by light codes into daily life is vital for Starseeds. This involves using the new insights and energies in enhancing personal growth, fulfilling their mission, and aiding in the collective evolution.

Ways to Utilize Light Codes

Creative Expression: Art, music, and writing can be mediums to express and further understand the information carried by light codes.

Service to Others: Utilizing the wisdom from light codes to help and guide others, especially in spiritual and healing practices.

Challenges and Solutions

While receiving light codes is a powerful experience, it can also bring challenges such as energetic overwhelm or difficulty in grounding these energies into the physical realm.

Overcoming Challenges

Community and Support: Engaging with a community of like-minded individuals can provide support and guidance in navigating these experiences.

Grounding Practices: Regular grounding exercises and spending time in nature can help in stabilizing the energies received.

Receiving light codes is a pivotal aspect of the Starseed's journey, offering profound insights and aiding in their spiritual evolution. Understanding and integrating these codes effectively can lead to a deeper connection with the cosmos and a more fulfilling execution of their mission on Earth.

Multidimensional Healing Modalities

Introduction to Multidimensional Healing

Multidimensional healing represents a holistic approach to wellness, transcending traditional methods by incorporating various dimensions of existence. Let's delve into these advanced healing modalities, exploring their significance for Starseeds navigating multiple realities.

Essence of Multidimensional Healing

Holistic Approach: It encompasses physical, emotional, mental, and spiritual aspects, addressing the interconnectedness of these layers in the healing process.

Transcendent Techniques: Utilizes techniques that go beyond the physical realm, tapping into higher dimensions and consciousness levels.

Key Modalities in Multidimensional Healing

Energy-Based Techniques

Reiki and Energy Work: Channeling universal life force energy to balance and heal the body's energy systems.

Crystal Therapy: Using crystals' vibrational frequencies to align and harmonize the body's energy centers.

Consciousness-Based Practices

Guided Meditation and Visualization: Techniques to access higher states of consciousness and promote deep internal healing.

Past Life Regression: Exploring past incarnations to understand and heal current life issues.

Integration with Starseed Missions

Multidimensional healing is not only a personal journey but also integral to a Starseed's mission. By achieving balance and wellness on all levels, Starseeds can more effectively fulfill their roles in elevating planetary consciousness.

Application in Mission Work

Self-Healing: Maintaining personal balance and health to serve as effective conduits for higher energies.

Healing Others: Using their heightened abilities to assist others in their healing journeys, contributing to collective healing.

Challenges and Navigating Them

While multidimensional healing offers profound benefits, it can also present unique challenges, especially for those new to these concepts.

Overcoming Potential Hurdles

Navigating Unfamiliar Techniques: Seeking guidance from experienced practitioners or communities can be vital.

Balancing Between Realities: Maintaining grounding and balance while exploring higher dimensions of healing.

Multidimensional healing modalities offer a comprehensive approach to wellness for Starseeds, addressing the complex interplay of physical, emotional, mental, and spiritual dimensions. By integrating these practices into their lives, Starseeds can enhance their personal well-being and effectively contribute to their broader cosmic missions.

Integrating Hyperdimensional Aspects

Embracing the Multidimensional Self

In the journey of a Starseed, recognizing and integrating the multiple aspects of their being is crucial. Let's explore the process of unifying these diverse components to achieve a harmonious existence across various dimensions.

Understanding the Multidimensional Self

Multiple Facets: Starseeds often possess aspects or fragments of themselves existing in parallel dimensions or timelines.

Conscious Integration: Acknowledging and embracing these facets is key to holistic self-awareness and growth.

Methods of Integration

Meditation and Mindfulness

Guided Visualization: Techniques to visualize and connect with various dimensional aspects of oneself.

Mindful Awareness: Being present and aware helps in recognizing subtle influences of different self-aspects in daily life.

Energetic Practices

Chakra Alignment: Balancing the energy centers to facilitate the flow of energy between different dimensional aspects.

Energy Clearing: Using techniques like Reiki or sound healing to clear blockages hindering integration.

Challenges in Integration

Navigating Dissonance

Emotional Conflicts: Different aspects may carry their unique emotional baggage, leading to internal conflicts.

Identity Crisis: Recognizing and reconciling the presence of multiple selves can be disorienting initially.

Overcoming Integration Challenges

Seeking Guidance: Consulting with experienced spiritual mentors or healers can provide support and clarity.

Patience and Compassion: Understanding that integration is a gradual process requiring self-compassion and patience.

Practical Applications in Daily Life

Harmonious Living

Unified Decision Making: Making choices that resonate with all aspects of oneself, ensuring decisions are balanced and aligned.

Enhanced Perception: Integrated aspects can lead to heightened intuition and a deeper understanding of life experiences.

Contribution to Mission

Greater Cohesion in Purpose: A unified self is more effective in fulfilling the Starseed mission of elevating consciousness.

Sharing Wisdom: Integrated knowledge from various dimensions can be shared to assist others on their spiritual journey.

Integration of hyperdimensional aspects is a pivotal step for Starseeds in embracing their full potential. This process not only leads to personal growth and enlightenment but also amplifies their ability to contribute meaningfully to their mission. By acknowledging and harmonizing the multiple facets of their existence, Starseeds can navigate their journey with greater clarity, purpose, and fulfillment, making a profound impact across dimensions.

Preparing for Ascension Across Dimensions

Embracing the Ascension Process

Ascension, in the context of hyperdimensional starseeds, refers to the process of evolving to a higher state of consciousness. So let's take a deep dive into the preparation required for this pivotal transition, guiding starseeds to align with their highest potential across multiple dimensions.

Understanding Ascension

Evolving Consciousness: Ascension involves expanding one's awareness and vibrational frequency, transcending the limitations of physical and temporal constraints.

Multidimensional Impact: The ascension process affects not just the individual but also resonates across various dimensions and realities.

Key Steps in Preparing for Ascension

Inner Work and Self-Realization

Deep Introspection: Engaging in practices like meditation, journaling, and mindfulness to understand one's true self and purpose.

Healing Past Traumas: Addressing and healing emotional wounds and karmic patterns to release old baggage.

Expanding Conscious Awareness

Learning and Growth: Continually seeking knowledge and wisdom about the nature of reality and spiritual laws.

Experiencing Multidimensional Realities: Actively engaging with different dimensions through astral projection, lucid dreaming, and other practices.

Overcoming Challenges

Navigating the Ego and Fear

Ego Dissolution: Recognizing and transcending the ego's limitations to embrace a more unified, cosmic identity.

Overcoming Fear: Facing and releasing fears, particularly related to change and the unknown.

Balancing the Physical and Spiritual

Grounding Practices: Balancing spiritual practices with grounding activities to maintain a harmonious physical and etheric existence.

Physical Health and Well-being: Ensuring physical health is aligned and supportive of higher vibrational living.

Practical Applications in Daily Life

Living in Alignment

Conscious Living: Making choices that reflect one's highest self and purpose, including relationships, career, and lifestyle.

Service to Others: Engaging in acts of kindness and service, understanding the interconnectedness of all beings.

Community and Connection

Building Support Networks: Connecting with like-minded individuals for support, learning, and shared experiences.

Teaching and Sharing Knowledge: Imparting wisdom and insights gained on the path to assist others in their ascension journey.

The journey towards ascension is a deeply personal yet universally impactful experience. It requires dedication, inner work, and a willingness to transcend beyond the known limits of existence. For starseeds, this path is not just about personal enlightenment but also about aiding the collective consciousness in its evolutionary leap. By preparing adequately for this ascension, starseeds embody their role as harbingers of a new era of multidimensional awareness and cosmic harmony.

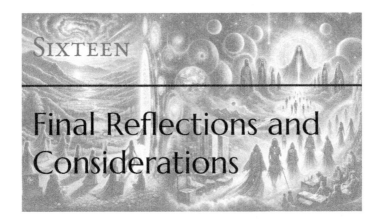

Sixteen
Final Reflections and Considerations

The Relevance of Ancient Wisdom

Unearthing Timeless Knowledge

So let's explore the profound connection between ancient wisdom and the journey of hyperdimensional starseeds. It underscores how timeless teachings provide invaluable insights for navigating the complexities of a multidimensional existence.

Understanding Ancient Wisdom

Defining Ancient Wisdom: Ancient wisdom refers to the spiritual knowledge and practices preserved through generations, often stemming from ancient civilizations and spiritual traditions.

Interconnection with Modern Consciousness: This wisdom, though ancient in origin, holds relevance and transformative power in contemporary hyperdimensional perspectives.

Core Tenets of Ancient Wisdom

Universal Laws and Principles

The Law of One: Emphasizing the interconnectedness of all existence and the unity of consciousness.

The Principle of Correspondence: 'As above, so below; as within, so without' – highlighting the mirroring of the macrocosm in the microcosm and vice versa.

Esoteric Knowledge and Practices

Sacred Geometry: Understanding the geometric codes and patterns that form the foundation of our reality.

Meditative and Mindfulness Practices: Techniques for inner peace and higher awareness that date back thousands of years.

Integrating Ancient Wisdom in Hyperdimensional Life

Personal Growth and Enlightenment

Self-Discovery and Enlightenment: Utilizing ancient teachings to foster self-awareness and spiritual awakening.

Navigating Life's Challenges: Leveraging the wisdom to deal with modern-day issues through a higher perspective.

Contribution to Collective Consciousness

Sharing Knowledge: Disseminating these ancient teachings to enlighten and uplift others.

Building a Conscious Community: Creating networks that uphold and propagate these age-old truths.

Challenges and Adaptation

Bridging the Gap

Contextual Relevance: Adapting ancient wisdom to the context of contemporary times while maintaining its core essence.

Overcoming Misinterpretations: Addressing and rectifying common misunderstandings about ancient teachings.

Preservation and Evolution

Preserving Ancient Knowledge: Safeguarding the purity of this wisdom through careful study and transmission.

Evolution of Wisdom: Allowing ancient knowledge to evolve and integrate with new spiritual insights and scientific understanding.

The relevance of ancient wisdom in the context of hyperdimensional starseeds cannot be overstated. It offers a treasure trove of knowledge and tools that aid in navigating multiple realities with awareness and grace. By embracing these teachings, starseeds can deepen their understanding of the universe and their role in it, contributing profoundly to their personal evolution and the upliftment of collective consciousness. In this cosmic journey, the ancients' insights serve as a guiding light, illuminating the path to transcendence and unity.

Our Cosmic Legacy

Embracing the Multidimensional Heritage

Now let's delve into the vast and profound concept of the cosmic legacy, a critical aspect of the hyperdimensional starseed's journey. This legacy encompasses not only our past but also the potential and responsibilities we carry into the future.

The Concept of Cosmic Legacy

Defining Cosmic Legacy: It refers to the rich tapestry of knowledge, experiences, and spiritual connections that starseeds inherit from the cosmos. This legacy transcends time and space, encompassing both ancestral wisdom and future possibilities.

Multidimensional Perspectives: Understanding that our legacy is not just about our linear past on Earth but also includes the wisdom and experiences from various dimensions and star systems.

Understanding Our Place in the Universe

Ancestral Connections

Star Lineages: Exploring the connections to various star systems and civilizations, such as Pleiadian, Arcturian, or Sirian, which many starseeds feel deeply connected to.

Learning from Galactic Ancestors: Drawing wisdom and lessons from these connections to enhance our understanding of our place in the cosmos.

Future Responsibilities

Custodians of the Earth: Emphasizing the responsibility of starseeds to nurture and protect the Earth, ensuring its vibrational ascension and well-being.

Guiding Humanity's Evolution: The role of starseeds in supporting the spiritual evolution of humanity, guiding them towards a more harmonious and enlightened existence.

Integrating and Honoring Our Legacy

Personal Integration

Embracing Galactic Heritage: Acknowledging and integrating the knowledge and strengths from our multidimensional selves.

Healing and Growth: Using our cosmic legacy for personal healing, growth, and the expansion of consciousness.

Collective Contribution

Sharing Wisdom: The importance of disseminating the ancient knowledge and cosmic insights for the betterment of all.

Building a New World: Contributing to the creation of a new earth that resonates with higher dimensions and values.

Challenges and Opportunities

Navigating Misunderstandings

Overcoming Skepticism: Addressing the challenges and skepticism faced in bringing forth this knowledge in a predominantly 3D world.

Balancing Between Worlds: Finding a balance between embracing cosmic legacies and functioning in the earthly realm.

Evolutionary Growth

Adapting Ancient Knowledge: Modifying and adapting ancient and cosmic wisdom to suit the needs of the current evolutionary stage of humanity.

Co-Creating the Future: Actively participating in the creation of a future that aligns with the higher vibrational frequencies.

Our cosmic legacy is not merely a heritage to be remembered; it is a living, evolving force that guides and shapes our journey as starseeds. By embracing and integrating this legacy, we step into our power as multidimensional beings, equipped to play a pivotal role in the ascension and evolution of consciousness, both on Earth and beyond. In doing so, we honor the past, enrich the present, and co-create a luminous future for ourselves and the generations to come.

The Great Cosmic Web: Interconnectedness

Understanding the Interconnected Universe

Now we'll explore the concept of the Great Cosmic Web and its significance in the lives of hyperdimensional starseeds. This vast, intricate web symbolizes the interconnectedness of all existence, spanning across multiple dimensions and realities.

Concept of the Cosmic Web

Definition and Nature: The Great Cosmic Web is a metaphorical representation of the interconnected network of energy, consciousness, and matter that binds the cosmos.

Manifestation Across Dimensions: It transcends physical space, manifesting through the subtle interplay of dimensions, from the physical to the ethereal.

Interconnectedness in Starseed Experience

Experiencing Unity

Feeling the Cosmic Connection: Starseeds often experience a profound sense of oneness with the universe, feeling deeply connected to various dimensions and life forms.

Enhanced Psychic Abilities: This interconnectedness often manifests through heightened psychic abilities like telepathy, clairvoyance, and astral projection.

Lessons from the Web

Learning from the Web's Harmony: Observing how different components of the Web work in harmony can offer profound insights into balance and unity.

Universal Empathy: The interconnected nature of the Web fosters a sense of universal empathy, allowing starseeds to feel the emotions and energies of others across dimensions.

The Role of Starseeds in the Cosmic Web

Nurturing the Web

Healers of the Web: Starseeds play a crucial role in healing and maintaining the integrity of the Cosmic Web, often intuitively identifying and repairing energetic disruptions.

Transmitters of Higher Frequencies: By channeling higher-dimensional energies, starseeds help in elevating the vibrational frequency of the Web.

Cosmic Diplomacy

Bridging Dimensions: Starseeds often act as bridges between different dimensions, facilitating the flow of knowledge and understanding.

Galactic Peacemakers: Their innate ability to navigate multiple realities positions them as peacemakers and mediators in interdimensional conflicts.

Practical Aspects of the Cosmic Web

Meditation and Visualization

Connecting with the Web: Techniques such as meditation and visualization can help starseeds to consciously connect with the Cosmic Web, enhancing their understanding and abilities.

Energy Work: Engaging in energy work like Reiki or Qi Gong can strengthen their connection to the Web, allowing for a more profound experience of interconnectedness.

Everyday Life

Integrating the Web's Wisdom: Bringing the lessons of the Web into daily life can transform relationships, work, and personal growth.

Conscious Living: Acknowledging the interconnectedness in everyday actions, starseeds can live more consciously, understanding the impact of their thoughts and actions on the wider Web.

Challenges and Opportunities

Balancing the Cosmic and Earthly

Staying Grounded: While exploring the vastness of the Cosmic Web, it's crucial for starseeds to remain grounded in their earthly existence.

Managing Sensitivities: The deep connection to the Web can sometimes be overwhelming, requiring starseeds to develop strategies to manage their sensitivities.

Contributing to the Web's Evolution

Co-Creating Reality: Starseeds play an active role in the evolution of the Web, contributing to the collective consciousness.

Visionary Leadership: With their unique perspective, starseeds are well-positioned to lead in the creation of a more interconnected and harmonious world.

The Great Cosmic Web represents the intricate tapestry of life and existence, binding everything in a delicate balance of energy and consciousness. For hyperdimensional starseeds, understanding and engaging with this Web is not just a journey of self-discovery but a sacred duty to maintain and enhance the harmony of the cosmos. Through their actions, thoughts, and spiritual practices, starseeds can strengthen this interconnectedness, fostering a greater sense of unity and empathy across all dimensions.

Transcending Limitations: A Final Word

Embracing the Infinite Potential

Let's dive into the profound experience of transcending limitations, a pivotal aspect of hyperdimensional existence. Starseeds, as beings aware of their multidimensional nature, are uniquely positioned to overcome the boundaries that confine conventional eof reality.

Understanding Limitations

Perceived Boundaries: Often, limitations are the product of societal, cultural, and personal beliefs ingrained in our consciousness.

Hyperdimensional Perspective: From a hyperdimensional viewpoint, these limitations are seen as mere illusions, part of a larger play of cosmic consciousness.

Overcoming Mental and Spiritual Barriers

Expanding Consciousness

Breaking Mental Constructs: Starseeds work to dismantle limiting mental constructs, replacing them with expansive, inclusive thought patterns.

Spiritual Growth: This involves deep spiritual work, including meditation, energy practices, and inner exploration, to realize one's true limitless nature.

Embracing Multidimensionality

Beyond Physical Constraints: Understanding that their essence transcends physicality, starseeds learn to navigate and integrate multiple dimensions.

Accessing Higher Knowledge: By doing so, they tap into a vast reservoir of wisdom and capabilities that lie beyond ordinary comprehension.

Harnessing the Power of Limitless Being

Activating Inner Potential

Inner Alchemy: Transformative practices enable starseeds to activate latent abilities, such as psychic powers and interdimensional communication.

Dynamic Creativity: Embracing their boundless nature, they can manifest realities and solutions that align with higher dimensional frequencies.

Living Beyond Fear

Conquering Fear: A significant part of transcending limitations is overcoming the fear that often accompanies the unknown or the unconventional.

Fear as a Teacher: Rather than a barrier, fear is viewed as a catalyst for growth, pushing starseeds to explore and conquer new horizons.

The Role in Cosmic Evolution

Agents of Change

Influencing the Collective: By transcending personal limitations, starseeds impact the collective consciousness, raising the vibration of humanity and the planet.

Inspiring Transformation: Their journey serves as an inspiration, showing others the potential that lies in transcending self-imposed boundaries.

Preparing for Future Shifts

Readiness for Dimensional Shifts: As the Earth and humanity approach significant evolutionary shifts, starseeds are at the forefront, prepared to navigate these changes.

Guiding Others: Their role includes guiding others through these transitions, using their knowledge and experiences to ease the process.

Practical Applications

Daily Practice

Mindfulness and Awareness: Incorporating mindfulness and self-awareness practices helps in recognizing and challenging limiting beliefs and behaviors.

Integration into Everyday Life: Transcending limitations isn't just a spiritual concept but a practical approach to living life more fully and authentically.

Community and Collaboration

Building Supportive Networks: Connecting with like-minded individuals and communities fosters an environment where transcending limitations is nurtured.

Collaborative Growth: Sharing experiences and insights contributes to a collective evolution, making the journey of transcendence a shared endeavor.

Transcending limitations is not just a concept but a lived reality for hyperdimensional starseeds. It is about realizing and embracing the infinite potential that exists within and beyond ourselves. This journey reshapes not only the individual but also has the power to transform the collective consciousness. As starseeds step into their limitless nature, they pave the way for a new era of consciousness, where boundaries are dissolved, and the true, boundless nature of existence is embraced.

Stepping into Your Hyperdimensional Power

Embracing Multidimensional Identity

The essence of a hyperdimensional journey is the realization and embodiment of one's multidimensional identity. This chapter explores how Starseeds, as hyperdimensional beings, fully step into their power, embracing the vastness of their existence.

Realizing the Multidimensional Self

Discovering Inner Universe: Starseeds come to understand that they are not just physical beings but encompass a multitude of dimensions and realities.

Integration of All Aspects: The journey involves harmonizing the physical, emotional, mental, and spiritual aspects, leading to a cohesive and empowered existence.

The Power of Hyperdimensional Consciousness

Expanding Beyond the Physical Realm

Beyond Physical Limitations: Recognizing their existence beyond the physical plane, Starseeds learn to operate within and influence multiple dimensions simultaneously.

Accessing Higher Realms: They tap into higher realms of consciousness, accessing wisdom and abilities that greatly surpass conventional human capabilities.

Mastery of Energy and Vibration

Manipulating Energy: With a profound understanding of energy dynamics, Starseeds master the art of energy manipulation for healing, transformation, and creation.

Vibrational Attunement: They align themselves with high-frequency vibrations, attracting experiences and entities that resonate with their elevated state.

The Role in the Cosmic Symphony

Earthly Missions and Galactic Responsibilities

Transforming the Earth: Many Starseeds are here to aid in Earth's transition into a higher vibrational state, bringing enlightenment and healing.

Galactic Contributions: Their responsibilities extend beyond Earth, contributing to the balance and evolution of the galaxy and beyond.

Guiding Humanity's Evolution

Influential Presence: By simply embodying their hyperdimensional nature, Starseeds influence and elevate the consciousness of those around them.

Mentorship and Guidance: They often take on roles of teachers and guides, helping others in their spiritual and multidimensional journeys.

Practical Application in Daily Life

Living as a Hyperdimensional Being

Mindful Living: Embracing a lifestyle that acknowledges and nurtures their multidimensional aspects in every action, thought, and interaction.

Harmonizing with the Universe: Staying in tune with cosmic rhythms and cycles, ensuring their actions are in harmony with the universal flow.

Impact Through Service

Service to Others: Recognizing their power, Starseeds use their abilities for the greater good, serving humanity and the planet.

Creating Positive Change: Their actions, grounded in love and wisdom, contribute to the creation of a more harmonious and enlightened world.

The Journey Forward

Continuous Evolution and Growth

Never-ending Expansion: The journey of a Starseed is one of perpetual growth and evolution, continually reaching for higher levels of consciousness and understanding.

Embracing the Unknown: Stepping into their power means being comfortable with the unknown, trusting that their path is divinely guided.

Preparing for Ascension

Ascension Process: As they advance, Starseeds prepare themselves for ascension, a process of transitioning to even higher dimensions of existence.

Role in Cosmic Ascension: Their personal ascension is part of a larger cosmic plan, contributing to the ascension of Earth and the collective consciousness.

Stepping into hyperdimensional power is about embracing the full spectrum of one's existence, from the physical to the highest realms of spirit. It's a journey of continuous discovery, growth, and service, leading not only to personal transformation but also contributing to the evolution of all. As Starseeds fully step into their power, they become beacons of light and wisdom, guiding humanity towards a brighter, more enlightened future.

Farewell and Bon Voyage: May Your Multidimensional Journey Be Filled With Light and Wisdom

As we conclude this exploration into the rich and complex world of hyperdimensional starseeds, we reflect on the transformative journey that has unfolded through these pages. This book has been a guide, a map, and a companion for those who find themselves navigating the multifaceted realities of a hyperdimensional existence.

The Journey Unveiled

Discovering the Hyperdimensional Self

Awakening to Multidimensionality: We began by introducing the concept of Starseeds and the multidimensional nature of reality, setting the foundation for understanding the hyperdimensional journey.

A Tapestry of Theories and Practices: From dimensional theory to the science of reality, we delved into the diverse aspects that comprise the hyperdimensional experience.

The Evolution of Consciousness

Expansion Beyond the Known

Transcending Limitations: Throughout the book, we emphasized the importance of transcending the perceived limitations of the physical realm, embracing the boundless nature of our existence.

Navigating Dimensions: We explored the practicalities and challenges of navigating multiple dimensions, emphasizing the importance of balance, grounding, and centeredness.

The Path of Service and Wisdom

Embracing a Higher Purpose

Galactic Missions and Earthly Roles: We touched upon the crucial roles Starseeds play in the cosmic plan, from healing missions to facilitating dimensional transitions.

Wisdom Sharing and Guidance: This journey is not just personal but also collective. Starseeds are called to share their wisdom, guiding others in their spiritual evolution.

Tools for the Hyperdimensional Traveler

Nurturing the Soul's Growth

Advanced Practices and Techniques: From meditation to astral projection, we provided tools to enhance the hyperdimensional experience, aiding in the personal and spiritual growth of Starseeds.

Maintaining Energetic Integrity: We discussed the importance of psychic protection, energy management, and maintaining vibrational harmony.

The Interconnectedness of All

Embracing the Great Cosmic Web

Understanding Our Place in the Universe: We emphasized the interconnectedness of all life, highlighting how each action and thought contributes to the greater cosmic web.

The Power of Collective Consciousness: The journey of a Starseed is intimately linked with the collective evolution of humanity and the universe.

Looking Forward

Stepping Into the Future

Continuous Evolution: The path of a Starseed is one of continual growth and evolution, a journey without end but filled with endless discoveries and joys.

Embracing the Unknown: With each step into the unknown, Starseeds expand the boundaries of what is possible, leading humanity into new realms of understanding and existence.

Parting Words

As we part ways at the conclusion of this book, it's important to remember that the journey of a Starseed is unique and deeply personal. It's a path filled with wonder, challenges, and profound transformation.

May your journey be illuminated with the light of wisdom and the warmth of universal love. Embrace your hyperdimensional power, and know that you are a vital part of a grand, cosmic symphony. Your journey is significant, your presence invaluable, and your potential limitless.

Farewell, dear traveler. May your multidimensional journey be an odyssey of enlightenment, filled with light, wisdom, and boundless possibilities. Remember, you are not alone in this vast universe; you are part of a greater whole, connected to all that exists. Bon voyage!

Printed in Dunstable, United Kingdom